Gift A

Gift A

More Memories
of
Reading

The publishers would like to thank the following companies for their

support in the production of this book

Main Sponsor

Goss & Co

The Abbey School

Broad Street Mall

Robert Darvall

Drews the Ironmonger

Foster Wheeler

Ernest Francis

G H Marshall

Johnson Matthey Plc

Thimbleby & Shorland

First published in Great Britain by True North Books Limited
England HX5 9AE
01422 377977

ISBN 1 903204 39 9

Text, design and origination by True North Books Limited
Printed and bound by The Amadeus Press Limited

More Memories of
of
Reading

Contents

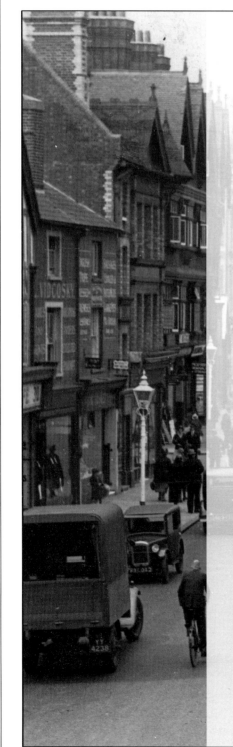

Introduction

Women proudly parade past the Town Hall in August 1941 to mark their contribution towards war work.

There is nothing wrong with self indulgence, absolutely nothing at all. Where is the harm in being pampered and who better to do it to you than yourself? This is your opportunity to wallow in nostalgia, to allow warm thoughts of yesteryear wash over you and take a moment to bask in the glow that sheer pleasure can bring. 'More Memories of Reading' is a book that will bring all those luscious feelings to the surface, packed as it is with a new collection of 20th century photographs that gloriously recall the days when cars rolled up to great department stores and trams dropped passengers off at little pubs along Friar Street and Broad Street. You are about to be whisked away on a magical mystery tour of the times that the reader and his parents can only half remember. Each image is supported by carefully written text, both wry and informative. Some of it is quite thought provoking, particularly when touching on the difficult days we endured when money was tight or the bombs were falling. Yet, from within it all, the spirit of Reading comes shining through as we relive the heritage that made our town a great place in which to be brought up.

The town of red brick, between the two rivers, has a long and illustrious past. Thousands of years ago, during the bronze and iron ages, people tilled the soil and hunted close by, but it is not until Saxon times, some 1,500 years back, that evidence of a settlement in Reading can be determined. Calleva, now Silchester, had been the main centre of population, but gradually Reading's influence grew. The town's name is derived from the followers of Reada (the red) and mention is made of Readingum during Aethelred and Alfred's battles with the invading forces of the Danes in 871. By the time the Domesday Book was compiled in 1086, the town's population had reached 500, but a major influence on its growth occurred when Henry I founded Reading Abbey in 1121. It was to dominate the town until Henry VIII's dissolution of the monasteries in the 16th century. Reading prospered during the intervening years as wool and cloth manufacture played an increasingly important role, becoming as significant as biscuit making was to be in the late 19th and early 20th centuries. In the 17th century the Civil War led to a slow down in the economy. Reading became a garrison town, supporting 3,000 troops faithful to the king. Its own population was only 6,000, so the strain on resources was quite severe. In April 1643 the Siege of Reading took place when Parliamentary troops attacked, eventually capturing the town and driving the Royalist forces back to Oxford.

In the 18th century the good times returned, partly thanks to Reading's easy access to the Thames and the Kennet. Great barges ploughed their way to and from London and the first sods were cut from the ground that would eventually form the Kennet and Avon Canal, opened in 1810, as a major link with Bristol. Roads were built or improved from the capital across to the west, making Reading an important coaching station and giving life to a number of coaching inns. With water and road links to Bristol and London established, the town could easily reach out to both sides of the country. At the beginning of the 19th century there were less than 10,000 people living here, but there were nearly six times as many who called Reading their home when the next century dawned. New industries, including Huntley and Palmer's biscuit works, Sutton's seeds, Simonds' brewery, engineering and brick

making, became major sources of wealth and employment. The coming of the railway in 1840 expanded horizons even further as businesses could now market their wares further and further afield.

Now we approach a time when we can start to tap into our personal memory banks - the 20th century. Although few readers can recall its early years, we all have relatives who gave us a glimpse of those days with their stories and grainy sepia photographs. 'More Memories of Reading' is the perfect companion to those half forgotten, semi-described reminiscences of life in the town as it developed during the last century. Glory in the fine buildings that our forefathers erected, only to be swept away to accommodate new roads and multi-storey car parks. Sniff the warm bread from the bakery, the sweet smell of loose Virginia in the tobacconist's and the gamey aroma of the rabbits hanging outside the butcher's shop. Try on a hat from a milliner or choose a suit from a fifty bob tailor, before you have to head off to a giant, impersonal shopping mall where some people have once entered, but have never been seen again. Examine the British built motor cars on

The Women's Land Army hold a recruitment drive in Market Place, 1940

Oxford Road, remembering when it was still simple to continue on into Broad Street, and enjoy a last waltz at the Majestic before strobe lighting and track sampling made dancing into a frenzy and not an art form. Whilst you do, make sure that there is a handkerchief nearby, because 'More Memories of Reading' does not gloss over the sadness that touches each and every one of us. Pause for quiet reflection with those gathered around the cenotaph, share the anguish of the loved ones recalling the horror of the bombing of the People's Pantry and join with the frustration of householders unable to hold back the floodwaters that the might of mother nature sends to try us. Every tear that is shed makes the joyous moments so much more precious. There are many of these on the following pages as memories of happy days come racing back. How we cheered and waved little union flags when royalty came to call, roared with laughter at the sound of Jimmy Edwards and the Glums in 'Take it from here' or purred with pleasure at the sight of that first postwar banana. Inside these covers is a world of nostalgia, the like of which the reader may feel should be shared by the whole family. It could

be a good excuse, too, for a cross generation get together, with everyone pooling memories, opinions and comment. Grannie was at school in the year we had three different kings on the throne and can recall that her mother mentioned that she was one of the flappers who danced the Charleston. Mum goes back to the days when dad walked her home from seeing Robert Redford, handsome and adventurous, in 'Butch Cassidy and the Sundance Kid', a smile playing on her lips as she nudges him about the cuddle they had on the back row. Even the children have their own nostalgic moments for the days of covering things with sticky backed plastic, playing with clackers and creating pictures with Fuzzy Felt. It will help the mood if the microwave is unplugged and crumpets are attached to the toasting fork, the wireless tuned to Dan Dare on Radio Luxembourg and training shoes put carefully to one side in favour of a sturdy pair of sensible brogues. Turn the first page, read the first caption and enjoy the thrill the initial photograph brings, secure in the knowledge that the same cosy tingle will be yours time after time as you move deeper into 'More Memories of Reading'.

The public toilets, the main focus of attention of the photographer in 1935, were an attractive feature of St Mary's Butts, at least at ground level, but their wrought ironwork has long since been dismantled and Readingers have to make their way inside the Broad Street Mall to spend a penny these days. One of the entrances to the modern complex of shops is where Holmes's store was trading all those years ago. Phone boxes and the little kiosk, selling snacks and light refreshments, are still in the same place, whilst a motor bike rank occupies the site of the nearest gents' entrance. The drinking fountain, at the far northern end of the block, has been retained, but as a modest flower bed. The tiny scooter on the left was an unusual sight in 1935, being more of an icon of the 1960s. Was the rider about to father a couple of Mods who would sweep down to Brighton or Bognor Regis, creating mayhem in battles with Rockers on Bank Holiday afternoons? Over to the right, the woman crossing the tramlines was heading for St Mary the Virgin, the oldest of the town's churches. Maybe she had a prayer to say for the poor Abyssinians whose country was about to be invaded by Italian troops, under the orders of the fascist dictator, Benito Mussolini.

Street scenes

Party politics were put on hold during World War II as MPs united in the national interest, though Labour and Liberal leaders stopped short of joining Neville Chamberlain's war cabinet. Two future prime ministers were brought back into the fold as Anthony Eden and Winston Churchill, both in the political wilderness for some years, accepted important posts. Chamberlain, an indecisive figure, was given the push when members of his own party rounded on him after a series of military debacles and Churchill took over the reins of government in May 1940. Six months later the ousted prime minister died, a broken man. With peace in Europe secure, the first general election for 10 years was held on 5 July 1945. The results were nearly all in when the current state of the parties was posted outside the Reading Standard newspaper office. In a shock result Labour swept to power in a landslide that gave the party 393 seats to the Tories' 213, with other parties capturing a mere handful of seats. Ian Mikardo won Reading for Labour with 30,465 votes, beating off the challenge of William McIlroy, the five time mayor, who polled 24,075 as a Churchill supporter. The Liberal, Tronchin-James, finished a distant third. Mikardo, a feisty left winger, claimed to have perfected a special way of recording the intentions of prospective voters, but he was the only one who appeared to understand it. He went on to become the Labour Party chairman in 1970.

Below: In the late summer of 1945 the station was decorated once again. It had flown its flags and aired its bunting on many occasions, celebrating national events. In the last 10 years there had been George V's silver jubilee, the coronation of George VI, VE Day and VJ Day, but on this occasion the station was ready to play its part in Reading's private homage to the 350 troops about to arrive on the platform. After three and a half years away, the Royal Berkshire Regiment was coming home from its service in the Far East. Mostly members of the 1st Battalion arrived that day, being warmly greeted by local dignitaries who wanted to thank them publicly for their service. But, their thoughts were not focused upon fine words, they wanted to be off and back into the bosoms of their homes and families. Servicemen were demobilised at the rate of 115,000 per week, with the aim of releasing

1,000,000 by December. Not everyone found it easy to adjust to the return to civvy street, having spent so long in uniform. Some brought with them stories about the atrocities in Japanese prison of war camps and the disease and starvation that killed thousands working as slave labourers on the railway line from Siam to Burma. Returning prisoners, all of them seriously emaciated, were the walking confirmation of man's inhumanity to man.

Bottom right: The no waiting sign was not meant to apply to those queuing for a trolley bus on the east side of St Mary's Butts in 1960. It was a forerunner of the double yellow lines, parking meters, one way systems and no go areas that would come to blight the life of the motorist in subsequent years. The two little girls under the awning were trying to persuade mum to buy them an ice cream and some sweeties for later. The choice was overpowering for them, as they considered strawberry, chocolate and vanilla flavours, topped off with delicious raspberry that was poured on as a mouthwatering liquid, not the congealed gel you get today. The ice cream was properly made to individual recipes that had a distinctive tang and was scraped into cornets or onto wafers with a wooden spatula. The modern stuff, squirted from soulless machines, is as insipid as a Donny Osmond smile. How lucky these children were to have something to tickle the taste buds and then be able to choose two ounces of sherbet lemons that would fizz on the tongue, chew their way through a penny Arrow bar and turn their tongues purple on some gentian violets. If mum was feeling generous she might even treat them to a comic where they could catch up with the latest adventures from Cactusville, as Desperate Dan munched through another cow pie.

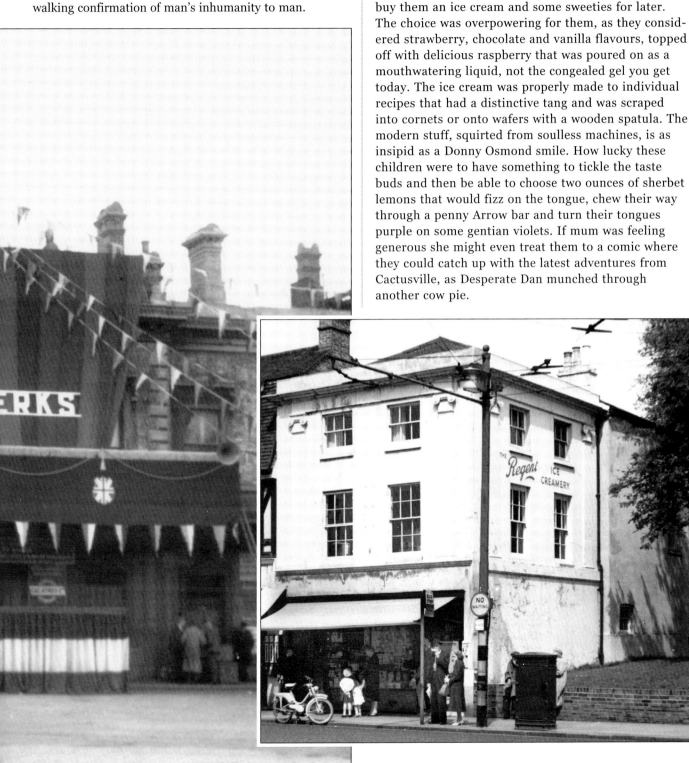

Below: There was a time when cars were parked on the ground, not miles up in the sky in high rise lots where you have to carry a ton of coins to meet the voracious appetite of the machines demanding, 'Feed me'. It may have been muddy underfoot as you left your car on what was to become the Butts Centre, but at least a shopper could remain solvent in 1965, rather than having to take out a second mortgage to pay the fees levied today. Looking at the rows of automobiles brings back to mind a time when the British car industry was heavily represented with Morris Minors, Triumph Heralds and Austin Princesses. There was nary a Japanese model in sight. This huge area, on the corner of St Mary's Butts and Oxford Road, was cleared of its mishmash of old shops and dwellings for redevelopment as a shopping complex that included a roof top car park, something of an innovation over 35 years ago. What was originally a novelty became something of a chore for motorists as they came to realise that they were tolerated, but at a price. The Butts Centre was opened in 1972, becoming known as the Broad Street Mall in 1987. In the distance, on the north side of Oxford Road, stands the former McIlroy's store. Its grand facade has been blighted by the logos of the various shops that have opened for business here in the last half century, but at least the main fabric remains, though what McIlroy would have thought about Blockbuster Video one shudders to think.

Right: Formerly the Public Hall, the office of the Reading Standard was photographed on the east side of London Street c1960. The weekly newspaper first went to press in 1891 and was still going strong when bought out by the Thomson empire and relaunched as the Reading Evening Post, moving its publication headquarters to Tessa Road. It became part of Berkshire Newspapers in 1989. Parked outside the office that day over 40 years ago was that symbol of perky youth, the BMC Mini, designed by Alec Issigonis, the son of a Greek merchant. He had been with Morris Motors since 1936 and had helped develop the very successful Morris Minor, but it was with this rival to the Volkswagen Beetle that he became a household name. The boxy, inexpensive, fuel-efficient Mini used a transverse engine to power its front wheels, a radical design at the time, comfortably seating four passengers despite being only 10 feet long. Its affordable price coincided with an upturn in the economy and an increase in the spending power of young people. By the time of his death in 1988, Issigonis had been made a member of the Royal Society, received a knighthood and seen sales of the car he designed reach 5,000,000. Who can ever see several Minis together without thinking of those that outstarred Michael Caine in the 1969 movie 'The Italian Job'?

This aerial view was taken from the south-east in 1930 at a time when this form of photography had become immensely popular. First used in a simple way during the first world war for reconnaissance purposes, bird's eye views of towns and the countryside gave people a perspective of their environment that was both novel and informative. The cameraman held the Huntley and Palmer factory and Reading Gaol in his viewfinder as he pressed the shutter. The famous biscuit business was established by Joseph Huntley in 1822, in conjunction with his son, Thomas, who baked the biscuits and confectionery whilst dad managed the business side. The Crown Inn was opposite their initial business, providing the Huntleys with access to the large numbers of passengers who made a brief stopover at the busy coaching inn. As there was insufficient time then to take a full meal, Huntley saw his opportunity in providing a snack to tide them over. He extended his service by packing his biscuits into tins to keep them fresh for the journey, and so the first seeds to greatness were sown. In 1841, after his father had retired through ill health, Thomas went into partnership with George Palmer, a man with similar strengths to Joseph. With Palmer's business acumen and Thomas Huntley's baking skills, the company flourished. Reading Gaol was immortalised by a former inmate, Oscar Wilde, who was incarcerated for two years in the 1833 prison designed by Sir Gilbert Scott and, on release in 1897, wrote 'The Ballad of Reading Gaol'.

The east side of Blagrave Street, in the early 1970s, leads up towards the municipal buildings where the museum, art gallery and town hall are situated. Several buildings had served as guild or town halls during Reading's history, including the onc built in 1786 that gave way to the distinctive buildings designed by Alfred Waterhouse, who was also responsible for Manchester Town Hall. Initially, the old assembly hall was retained, but this was supplanted by a delightful new one in 1882. The impressive brick and ornamental terracotta work was carried out by Collier's and the buildings were further extended in late Victorian times to include the additional facilities that are there today. Major refurbishment in the 1990s has ensured that these municipal buildings are amongst the most attractive in the land. Blagrave Street is named after John Blagrave, a notable benefactor who was a member of a wealthy Elizabethan family. This mathematician and scientist lived in Southcote, publishing the 1585 tome, 'The mathematical jewel'. After his death in 1611 his will, amongst other charitable bequests, provided funds that each year provided a wedding dowry for one poor servant girl, providing she had given good service for a minimum of five years. He is buried in St Laurence's Church, on the far side of the Town Hall.

Left: St David's Hall, on the south side of London Road, was one of the halls of residence established when the University of Reading was founded on 17 March 1926. It still functions today, though the Gyosei College took over the hall and extensively modernised its 102 rooms, re-opening in 1991. Students who lived here in previous generations will regard those studying in the 21st century as being somewhat pampered. All the rooms are single units, fully centrally heated, having both telephone and television facilities, all but 28 being equipped with a private bath or shower. There are microwaves all over the building, a far cry from the toaster, kettle and occasional gas ring that were there before. The university is the only one established in Great Britain between the wars and came into being largely thanks to its connections with Oxford. Some of that university's lectures were first delivered in Reading in 1885, leading to the establishment of the University Extension College in 1891. The Royal Charter to found the University of Reading was granted in May 1925, receiving royal assent on the following year, but it outgrew the site around St David's and relocated to Whiteknights Park after World War II. Today, the hall is home to a large number of Japanese students, giving it an international and cosmopolitan feel.

Below: Looking eastwards towards Caversham Bridge on a balmy day in 1960, the little girls cooled their toes in the gentle waters of the Thames. Elsewhere, people rowed, paddled or punted their craft as they enjoyed the pleasures of water sports. The air was only disturbed by the occasional phut-phut of a small motorboat as it eased its way downstream. Families picnicked on potted meat sandwiches, washed down with a bottle of Simonds' ale or a swig of Kiaora orange juice. They gazed upon the bridge that had had been opened by the Prince of Wales, the future Edward VIII, on 25 June 1926. Plans for building a new crossing over the river had been afoot for some time, but were delayed by the onset of World War I. In 1911 Reading had been granted permission to extend its boundaries to include Caversham, much to the disgust of some of the latter's residents who enjoyed the independence afforded by a separate village. One proviso of the changes was that a new bridge had to be built, affording better access to the rest of the borough, as the 1869 iron bridge was much too narrow. That had taken the place of one first seen in 1231, though it was badly damaged in the Civil War and piecemeal repairs down the years had left it a hotchpotch of stone, brick and timber.

Events & occasions

In recent years it has been necessary to book celebrities to attract crowds to the official opening of a new store, but on 1 September 1928 the mayor was enough of a draw to pack the Cheapside pavement. The new central premises of the Reading Industrial Co-operative Society had grown from the small enterprise founded by Stephen Gyngell, a 28 year old apprentice at Reading Ironworks. He had been encouraged by the success of the first co-operative enterprise of the Equitable Pioneers in their little shop in Toad Lane, Rochdale in the mid 1800s. Before long the country was awash with customers seeking to earn their 'divi'. Cheapside is normally a name associated with ancient markets, not unlike the 'Chipping' of many towns in the Cotswolds, but the connection for Reading is out of keeping with this pattern. Cheapside was only given its name about 100 years ago and there has never been a market on this site. As the mayor addressed the gathering, perhaps he thought that he might be able to secure some extra votes when the next elections came along. Women had been given limited voting rights after World War I, but it was not until 1928 that they were fully enfranchised. The bill granting universal suffrage was passed just weeks before the death of Emmeline Pankhurst, the founder of the Women's Social and Political Union.

Taking the salute at the cenotaph in the grounds of Brock Barracks, Oxford Road, on 11 November 1927 the men of the Royal Berkshire Regiment gave homage to the men who had paid the ultimate sacrifice in the defence of their country. The regiment had been based here since 1878 and although this memorial was erected in memory of those who lost their lives in the first world war, it is not the only Reading memorial marking the fine service this regiment has given. The Maiwand Lion in Forbury Gardens honours the 328 officers and men killed in the Afghan Campaign of 1879-80. Then called the 66th (Berkshire) Regiment of Foot, formed in the 18th century, it combined with the 49th (Princess Charlotte of Wales) Regiment in 1881, as the 2nd Battalion, Princess Charlotte of Wales (Berkshire Regiment). In 1920 it was renamed the Royal Berkshire Regiment, but titles meant little to those lost in their own memories of comrades who had fallen on foreign fields. There were 6,688 to be remembered, a huge figure that stops us in our tracks today as we try to cope with the thought of how that size of carnage must have affected the local population. Every single family lost at least one relative in the war that was supposed to end all wars.

During the 1926 royal visit to Reading the bystanders outside the Great Western Hall were treated to a display by the remarkably named Australian Scottish Ladies Pipe Band. As if it were not bad enough that, in a couple of years' time, the Aussies would unleash Don Bradman upon us, these women had taken over the instrument that was the pride and joy of our cousins north of the border. At least they could claim Scottish ancestry as they embarked on their world tour, but the skirl of 'Waltzing Matilda' being fingered on the chanter had a few 'bravehearts' turning in their graves. One Glaswegian looking on was heard to mutter something unkind about learning to play whilst they whiled away the hours on the convict ships en route to Botany Bay. His comments were quickly silenced by those who reminded him of the sacrifices the Anzacs made at Gallipoli on behalf of the British Empire in April 1915. The sight of all women bands was still new to the general public that had yet to grant full voting rights to the fairer sex. Even after that milestone was passed, in much later years the Ivy Benson Band playing in a dance hall or the Dagenham Girl Pipers entertaining at half time during a soccer match were still something of a novelty.

Left: Two days previously, on 23 June 1926, Edward, Prince of Wales, had celebrated his 32nd birthday before setting off for a round of official functions that included this visit to Palmer Park. His modern, snappy style of dress contrasted with the more mundane, old fashioned look of those flanking him. High winged collars, watch chains in the waistcoat pocket and spats around the ankles were the fashion of previous decades. The British public took its clothing lead from royal role models more than film stars in the 1920s, for was not this the man who was to invent the Windsor knot for our neckties? He did bow to some conformity in wearing a bowler, but David, as his family called him, would have been happier in a panama or homburg and more comfortable still, bare headed. The park where he accepted the applause of the crowd had been donated by George Palmer JP, the Member of Parliament for Reading (1878-1885). A partner in the biscuit firm that was one of the town's largest industries, he was also a notable benefactor, giving 14 acres of land by the Thames for use as a public recreation ground. In 1890 he followed this up by presenting the 49 acre Palmer Park, to the east of the town, for sports and recreational use. Palmer even paid for the railings and tree planting.

Below left: In 1926, when the Prince of Wales arrived on the royal train, the red carpet was rolled out across the platform of Reading Station. As the stationmaster and civic dignitaries greeted him, he politely doffed his hat, as he always did. This was something of a trademark for the heir to the British throne, illustrating the impeccable manners of the urbane prince. The motorcade carrying him from the station was immediately hailed by cheers from the massed multitudes lining the approach and all the way along the streets into the town centre. The official opening of Caversham Bridge was one of the official duties he was to carry out that day, something he should have undertaken the previous month. However, the general strike in May had put a stop to that as the country ground to a standstill, but here he was, several weeks later, and the public roared its approval. The railway came to the town in 1840 and the remarkable 19th century engineer, Isambard Kingdom Brunel, built the first Reading Station. As the townspeople lived to the south of the tracks, both the up and down platforms were quaintly built on that side. This Great Western station is a happy survivor of the changing face of Reading, still serving passengers, but with refreshment rather than tickets, as the Three Guineas. The new one, standing alongside the old, was opened by the Queen in 1989.

Top: The procession of the Ancient Order of Foresters passed along Broad Street en route to the High Court service at St Mary's Church on Sunday, 31 July 1927. Proudly displaying their chains of office and ceremonial regalia, the top hatted bigwigs included the High Chief Ranger, in the front centre, accompanied by the secretary, Stanley Duff, on the left. Other members of the council followed in their wake. The procession was over 1,200 strong and took an age to wend its way past the crowds lining the streets. The watchers showed their social standing by the kind of headgear they wore, with firmly pulled down cloche hats for the fashion conscious women, flat caps for working class men and trilbies and homburgs for the more upwardly mobile males. Refreshment stalls, dotted along the route, did a roaring trade as the Foresters celebrated the traditions of a society that dated back to 1878. There was a section for youngsters as well, called the Royal Berkshire Juvenile Foresters. Numbering a membership of 1,500, they paraded in the wake of the main procession. We loved watching and participating in shows of unity and membership, but you would have thought the public would have had its fill of marching, less than a decade since the Great War had finished. Many marched in that period for the last time.

Above right: Queen Victoria looked down from her perch outside the Town Hall, where she had been positioned to mark her 1887 golden jubilee, and thought, 'Here we go again'. The year had only been three weeks old when her great grandson, Edward, had been proclaimed king and here she was, watching another announcement with just three weeks of 1936 left to run. Another great grandson was, this time, the subject of the ceremony. Edward VIII had split opinion in the country over his affair with Wallis Simpson, the twice divorced American socialite. Whilst most might have forgiven his dalliance as a

popular Prince of Wales, to declare his intention to marry and make her his queen was too much for many to stomach. The government and church were firmly against the union, though news of the liaison was kept from the general public for some time. When the storm broke, debate raged wildly about the duty of a monarch, on one side, and the right of a man to choose his love, on the other. Pressure from his advisers to send Mrs Simpson packing was too much for the King to bear and he abdicated before ever being crowned. Outside the Town Hall the proclamation of his successor, George VI, was read to a packed assembly who rallied to the cause, throwing public support behind the man who would heal the rift and reign for the next 15 years.

Far right: Women paraded and waved the flag with great pride as they passed the Town Hall in August 1941 on their celebratory walk marking their contribution towards war work. It was arranged partly to acknowledge their value, but also as a recruitment drive to attract more women to their ranks. For any who were worried about getting their hands dirty, they were reminded that contact with greasy and oily machines was no worse than washday red and the havoc on the skin created by the drudgery of housework. Those who opted for factory work found jobs ranging from making ammunition to

manufacturing aeroplanes, often working long hours. Some had to relocate to find employment, but skilled women could earn over £2 15s (£2.75) a week. Although this was a good wage for females, it was still less than their male counterparts and led to some dissatisfaction, perhaps the forerunner of the equality thrust of later years. Women who worked the land had a more difficult time, especially in winter, when conditions were poor. Sometimes they had to break up the earth by hand, ready for sowing, but they tended to eat better than their town cousins as there was a plentiful supply of wild animals available. Hares, rabbits, pheasant and partridge were frequent visitors to the pot and Land Army girls had a healthy and rosy glow to their cheeks.

Left: On the weekend following the announcement that the war in Europe was over a victory parade was held to celebrate the occasion. The Mayor of Reading, Alderman WW Newman, took the official salute, though not everybody gave full approval to the show of unity and the merriment that followed the ceremonial events. War was still being waged in the east and many of our forces were still engaging the enemy as the march past was happening. As thousands were unaccounted for in foreign prisoner of war and labour camps and soldiers were still falling in the battlefield, some felt that the scenes of rejoicing were insensitive. However, the majority could not hold back its excitement and relief that the bombs had stopped falling on our homeland and that the war in Europe was over. Bonfires were lit on the hillside and in some streets. People danced the conga down Friar Street and hokey cokeyed in the Forbury. Complete strangers grabbed one another in bear hugs and planted slobbering kisses on any uniformed person they came across. Hats were thrown into the air as successive sets of three cheers were called for. There was some sympathy for those who still had loved ones fighting in the Pacific and the Burmese jungle, but it was impossible to stem the tide of joy that swept across Britain in May 1945 as VE Day was celebrated with gusto.

Below: Looking elegant in her splendid hat, one of the best loved figures of the 20th century was taking a keen interest in the parcels being prepared at the Army Comforts Depot in St Mary's Butts in August 1944. Queen Elizabeth, wife of George VI, quickly established herself in the hearts of the British public. As Elizabeth Bowes-Lyon, her marriage to the Duke of York in 1923 was widely applauded by a population tired of a diet of foreign princesses and noblemen marrying into our royal family. The impressive way in which she supported and shielded her nervous husband when he was thrust onto the throne after the abdication of Edward VIII further enhanced her reputation. But, it was to be the war that cemented her place in our affections. She refused point blank to run away with her family to the safety of Canada, declaring that her place was with her people. When Buckingham Palace was bombed her stock increased even more, stating that she could now look a blitz sufferer from London's East End in the face. Here she examined knitwear, cigarettes, chocolate, games and mouth organs that were gifts for the frontline troops. She included tins of sweets her elder daughter, had sent. After the sad death of the king in 1952 she became affectionately known as the 'Queen Mum' and it remains a national disgrace that the government did not mark her 100th birthday in August 2000 as an official day of celebrations.

Although victory in Europe was announced to excited crowds in London by Winston Churchill on the afternoon of 8 May 1945, it was not until the following Saturday that many street parties were held to celebrate VE Day. By then precious ration coupons had been sacrificed with gay abandon so that the day could go with a swing. Margarine was carefully spread on the sandwiches before a thin layer of jam was added. The store of egg powder was raided to make the little buns and cakes that were necessary for any good party. Trestle tables, borrowed from the church or schoolroom, were dragged into the middle of the street and table decorations appeared as if from nowhere. Times may have been hard, but no party tea could be had without the table being properly set and adorned with vases of flowers and tiny posies. Catherine Street, off Oxford Road, had its reminders of what the residents had gone through in the form of the air raid shelters that were still on the side of the road. Take note of the handful of men pictured here. They are middle aged, not a young chap in sight. The war in Europe was officially over, but our boys were still in uniform, mopping up or engaged in the war against Japan, anxiously awaiting the day when they would be reunited with their families.

Left: Although he had no local connection, Garnet Street owes its name to Garnet Joseph, 1st Viscount Wolseley (1833-1913), a soldier who was best known for his army reforms. He saw action in the second Anglo-Burmese War, the Crimean War and the Indian Mutiny before earning a knighthood after leading a successful expedition in the Gold Coast against the Ashanti in 1874. He became a minor national hero when his exploits were recounted in the press. In keeping with the Victorian tradition of naming places after military figures, there are a number of Garnet Streets in our towns, including one as far away as Middlesbrough. The one in Reading held its VE Day party on 8

May 1945, when there was much jollity as gay bunting was stretched across the road as an accompaniment to the banners and flags that appeared for the first time since the coronation of George VI eight years earlier. Guests of honour at the table were two GIs, members of the United States armed forces stationed in Britain who fought their way across the Normandy landing beaches with us in June 1944. This pair must have found Britain a pleasant surprise, for their presence in their own country's army was greeted with hostility by some of the rednecks who believed in segregation. Treated with a respect and given a warm welcome they could not expect in Alabama or Georgia, the black GIs returned home singing the praises of the hospitable British. At home they could not even sit on a bus near a white man, yet in Reading they shared his table.

Below left: The event that made the world tremble at the thought of nuclear weapons being unleashed on a global scale took place on 6 August 1945, when an atomic bomb was

dropped on the Japanese military port of Hiroshima. A specially equipped B-29, the 'Enola Gay', unleashed its cargo, destroying most of the city, and estimates of the number killed have ranged from 70,000 to 80,000. Deaths from radiation poisoning have mounted through the subsequent years, blighting the lives of families for decades. Three days later, a second bomb wiped out 40,000 more in Nagasaki in western Kyushu. Emperor Hirihito surrendered his country on 14 August, to the comment from the American president, Harry Truman, 'This is the day

we have waited for since Pearl Harbour.' The following day a crowd gathered by Reading Town Hall to hear the news from the mayor, who had just been attending the service of thanksgiving in St Laurence's Church. The government declared a two day national holiday and celebrations for the victory over Japan rivalled those held three months earlier when Germany had been defeated. As the onlookers listened to the mayor's address being relayed over the tannoys, how many gave a thought to the immense power that was now in the hands of the military? It meant that we were about to enter the period of the cold war, when the great nations targeted one another with weaponry that could kill millions and the threat of a nuclear war hung over our heads like an evil spectre.

Bottom: On Shinfield Road, VJ Day in August 1945 was marked by a party and fancy dress parade. Even the adults joined in on the act, dressing up with as much fervour and invention as that shown by the children. The festivities were partly down to relief that the war was fully over at last, but they were also rejoicing for the freedom that had been won for the next generation. The angelic little tots pictured here will be looking for their bus passes before too long. What sort of memories do they have of the day they got dressed up and smiled for the camera, each one hoping to have won a prize? Typical of boys the world over, one lad seems to be more interested in the contents of the small truck in front of him. Never mind posing coquettishly for the photographer, like his pretty sisters, there might be something worth playing with inside here. If so, it would not be some electronic piece of gadgetry that fascinates 21st century children, but something simpler, but just as interesting. It could be a handful of marbles, a top and whip, a monkey on a stick or a skipping rope. Youngsters' playthings have changed so much since those days, for when did you last see a child mark out the pavement for hopscotch, start a game of elastics or play two ball against a gable end?

Above: Tea up! What a cheering sight that was for the residents marooned in their bedrooms during the floods of 1947. The volunteer from the Women's Voluntary Service (WVS) waded through the floodwaters, bringing what help she could. Over 1,600 houses were badly hit, Caversham being particularly affected, as mother nature wreaked her havoc on a population that had avoided the worst excesses of German bombing during six years of war. Rain seemed more potent than high explosive as householders ran out of fresh drinking water and food floated off downstream, having been washed out of larders. Fresh supplies were hoisted up on ropes and in buckets as relatives and the voluntary services came to help where they could. The WVS was well versed in the art of providing support, for its members had been running refreshment vans, clothing centres and salvage clearing houses throughout the war as an integral part of the civil defence measures. No shrinking violets, these women went where it hurt, straight in at the sharp end as fires raged following a bombing raid, putting the needs of others first. Formed in 1938, the organisation was the brainchild of Stella, Lady Reading, who had been at the heart of the Personal Service League of the early 30s that helped families adversely affected by the depression years. The WVS gained official royal approval in 1966, becoming the Women's Royal Voluntary Service.

As surely as night follows day, the big freeze of the winter of 1947 brought, in its aftermath, the troubles of the big thaw. For months we had shivered in the cold, made worse by coal shortages and power cuts. When the temperature rose in April, the ice and snow swelled rivers to an extent that hardly any part of the country escaped from the inevitable floods that followed. The Thames rose 15 inches and burst its banks, badly affecting a large area around Caversham Road and Vastern Road. Here, on Great Knollys Street, families put a brave face on it, pretending to enjoy the boat trip for a marooned grandma getting a piggyback ride into the craft that would take her off to dry land. Sodden carpets, water-logged furniture and a layer of mud that stank to high heaven would be the greeting to which she returned. The School Meals' Service and the British Restaurant on Kings Road, ably supported by the WVS and other volunteers, worked hard in ferrying hot meals to stranded householders. The mayor, Alderman Phoebe Cusden, rolled up her sleeves and weighed in as well. A distress fund raised £12,000 for the 200 families who had to be evacuated and those who lost many precious possessions in the worst flooding since 1894. It was a week before the water level fell and months before normality returned.

A wet and gloomy day on Broad Street in 1963 did not seem to dampen the spirits of those watching or taking part in the annual Rag Day parade, though the bobbies in their capes probably wished for drier duties. Students during rag week got up to all sorts of pranks, but as they were conducted in the pursuit of raising funds for charity, the police usually turned a blind eye. After all, the odd outsize bra draped across the front of Queen Victoria's statue or a huge nappy on the Maiwand Lion might have offended some, but they did not hurt anyone. Dignitaries were 'kidnapped' and the ransom paid for their release swelled the charity coffers. One of the most amusing stunts in previous years was when two future pillars of society dressed up as a pantomime cow and presented themselves for auction at the cattle market. This year, as the Beatles had their first number one hit record with 'From me to you', the students claimed a record of their own, knitting a 280 foot scarf, comfortably eclipsing an earlier effort by a Canadian university. The trolley bus making its way past the procession of floats had only another five years of service left as it would make its final journey on 3 November 1968. Particularly useful during the petrol shortages of the war years and at the time of the Suez crisis, a lack of manoeuvrability caused their downfall. It was ironic that this was the reason given for phasing out the trams they had replaced.

Below: Council workmen and officers in their business suits look rather precariously poised on the gangplank and ladders in place outside the Town Hall in late May 1953. The finishing touches were being put to the decorations that would honour the coronation of our queen on 2 June 1953. It was a momentous time, not just for her, but across the world as representatives from the far corners of the British Commonwealth flooded into London to pay homage to Her Majesty. One of the most impressive figures was that cut by Queen Salote of Tonga, a huge and beaming figure, who waved vigorously to the crowds as her open carriage rapidly filled with rainwater pouring down upon her. Her spirits were not dampened, nor were those of the crowd who gave her a rousing ovation as she drove past on her way to the Abbey. On the eve of Coronation Day our hearts had been lifted by the exciting news released from Kathmandu. New Zealander Edmund Hillary and a local Sherpa, 'Tiger' Tensing, had been the successful members of Colonel John Hunt's expedition to climb Everest. This was to be one of the most memorable of years. We had our new queen, the unclimbable had been conquered, Stanley Matthews won his FA Cup medal, Gordon Richards rode a Derby winner and the England cricket team regained the Ashes.

A car to Khartoum

When a stranger's car broke down outside the offices of Reading insurance broking firm Goss & Co. employee Michael King offered the man the use of a phone to summon help.

Michael refused to accept payment for the call, but instead said he would like to quote for his car insurance when his policy was due for renewal.

The man happily agreed and subsequently swapped insurance firms. Years later the company he had helped to found, by then a listed company with branches in Europe and Africa, would become Goss & Co.'s largest client.

Michael King would, in turn, have become the Managing Director and Chairman of a group of companies with a turnover which would exceed £20 million.

The fact is that we all need insurance for one reason or another and buying our policies through an experienced and knowledgeable independent broker makes sense. After all, how on earth are we poor ignorant souls able to distinguish between the hundreds if not thousands of confusingly packaged products offered by a multitude of insurance companies? We need the help of experts not simply to get value for our money but to get the kind of insurance product we need.

Goss & Co. has its roots firmly planted in Reading having been established here in 1921. It set out to offer exceptional solutions to an exclusive area and today it prides itself on its local focus, specialising in risk management consultancy and insurance solutions to business clients mainly within a 50 mile radius of the town.

Limiting its geographical area has far from limited the company's abilities. Being the largest independent insurance brokers in the Thames Valley the firm's clients

Top left: Captain Ernest Goss, founder of Goss & Co, 1921. Right: Presenting a cheque to the charity Readibus Ltd in 1985.

receive the highest standard of care. And it is still growing and improving; through acquisitions it is now large enough to negotiate the best possible terms for clients but still small enough to offer a personal service.

As the business has grown so has its profile, through its ethos of providing first class assistance whether to an individual client with modest needs or to a blue chip business with far larger demands remains exactly the same.

The modern business of the Goss Group in fact involves five firms: Goss & Co. (Insurance Brokers) Ltd, Goss & Co. (Financial Services) Ltd, both trading as Goss & Co., John Holt & Partners, Travel Incorporate and Brooking Travel.

GOSS & Co

Goss & Co. was founded in 1921 by two prominent members of the local community: Captain Ernest E Goss and William Goss.

Captain Goss was a master mariner and one of the last men to have sailed around Cape Horn on board a commercial clipper - and indeed such a sailing ship figured prominently on company stationery from 1921 to 1973 and a more stylised version is still the company's logo for its insurance broking and financial services divisions. Ernest's brother William Goss, who was Mayor Elect at the time of his death, had originally been manager of The Ocean which is now part of Norwich Union.

William Goss' two sons Stanley and Philip Goss would eventually become the second generation of the Goss family to run the firm.

Through the ensuing years the company would provide a first rate personal and professional service as local agents to many of the insurance companies of the day which have since become household names.

The Goss business began from premises in Butter Market in a building which would suffer heavy damage during the second world war when one of the few bombs dropped on Reading fell there. The bombing meant that new premises were needed and a move was made to the Oddfellows Hall which would subsequently become Marks and Spencer.

In 1981 the Goss organisation was restructured to clearly define each area of business; clients could then more readily identify who should respond to their needs.

Three subsidiary companies were established. Each of the three companies had its own management team, staffing and premises, as well as total accountability to its clients.

Top: *Goss & Co (Insurance Brokers) Ltd, staff pictured in their offices in Clarendon House.*
Above: *Thanks to the latest technology Chris Alderton has the entire mortgage market at his fingertips. Goss & Co (Financial Services) Ltd.*

Goss & Co. (Insurance Brokers) Ltd would be in the business of commercial insurance and the personal business of commercial clients. Goss & Co. (Life & Pension) Brokers Ltd would provide experienced independent financial advice for its own client portfolio as well as advising the clients of other Group Companies and professional advisers. Thirdly, JE Mayler & Co. Ltd would be concerned with Personal Business not dealt with by the rest of the group.

In 1984 the group took its first step outside its traditional area of business by acquiring MWF Carter Ltd holiday and business travel agents operating then from Kings Road and a member of ABTA and registered with IATA.

By the close of the millennium Goss & Co. had become the largest independent insurance broker in the Thames Valley growing at an annual rate of 17-20 per cent each year with an annual turnover of more than £9 million.

Sophisticated IT systems ensure that quotes, cover notes, proposals and payment can be dealt with in the same time as a direct seller.

Top left: *Michael King, chairman, presents the new corporate image of Goss & Co.* ***Right:*** *St Laurence House, home to Goss & Co (Financial Services) Ltd.*

Against the trend of many insurance companies to outsource the handling of claims, particularly motor, Goss & Co. deals with claims itself. In the event of a claim the broker who placed the policy will also be the person handling the claim - and, of course, at no extra cost to the client.

At their offices in Queens Road the 50 plus insurance broking staff are looking forward to increasing business even further with the company mounting campaigns to make the business community even more aware of its services. Growth has come mainly from new business gained through personal recommendation.

Meanwhile at St. Laurence House in the Forbury, bought by the group in 1991, the Life and Pensions business, now styled Financial Services, has also grown rapidly. Indeed, Goss & Co. (Financial Services) are now also recognised as one of the leading firms in the area. St. Laurence House suits them very well offering their clients consulting rooms situated conveniently in the town centre and, coincidentally, only a "stones throw" from Goss's first offices some 80 years ago.

Captain Goss and his brother William would no doubt be thrilled to see the firm they launched so long ago sailing profitably into the next century, its stationery still bearing a sailing ship logo on its letterheads. Goss & Co. has weathered the storms and choppy water of countless economic booms and recessions but unlike many of its early competitors survived and grew by always putting the safety and security of its clients above all other considerations.

John Holt & Partners

In 1963 the Beatles dominated the pop charts, beer was 1s 4d a pint (7p) and a terraced house or a maisonette cost less than £3,000. On April Fools Day in that year Jack Holt entered the financial services business. Today, now as part of the Goss group, the firm is still going strong.

Originally the vast majority of business was centred around the home mortgage market at a time when independent advice was hard to come by. Over the years the firm would expand into a much wider range of financial services: retirement planning, commercial insurance broking, pension schemes and investment.

Jack Holt founded the business after doing his stint of National Service in the RAF and training with Norwich Union and city brokers Norman Frizzell.

The new firm began its life in premises at 147 Friar Street where it would stay for nine years.

Back then the office still used mechanical typewriters and mechanical calculators. Today state of the art computer software for business processing, clients' records and accounts have long since replaced the clattering comptometers and tapping typewriters we remember so well from the 1960s.

The decade of the 1960s was a boom time for housing in Berkshire with lots of firms relocating to the area and there were many opportunities for a mortgage broking business to grow. Many new people came to live in the area but despite the influx of new faces there would be a strong emphasis on local recruitment. Jack Holt took pride in mainly choosing people to work for the firm who were already known and who had worked for local insurance companies, banks and building societies.

A big step forward in 1970 was when Stuart Crippen joined Jack having trained and gained valuable experience with both Phoenix and Equity & Law Assurance Companies. Soon after in 1972 John Holt & Partners moved to Greyfriars House: the move involved a big hike in rent and a commensurate increase in responsibility to increase business to pay it. Such confidence in the future was not misplaced. Increased activity through the 1970s and 80s would more than cover the cost of larger premises.

By the 1990s however it was the investment side of the firm which was growing more rapidly rather than mortgages and insurance. The country was beginning to see people starting to inherit from the first main era of home ownership. Money was beginning to cascade down to people who would not have been investors 20 years earlier and who now needed independent financial advice.

And it was not just individuals who looked to John Holt & Partners for advice; work included corporate employee benefit schemes such as pensions, life assurance and health schemes. For example, many local software houses, which had spun off from giant American corporations, sought advice from the firm.

All the firm's team of authorised financial advisers have been in the financial services business all their working lives and their experience and know-how is second to none.

One of the few limits to further growth was finding the right people. The firm could easily increase its market share, but sourcing first class advisers and support staff was proving more difficult.

Above: *Partners Jack Holt (second right), Stuart Crippen and Peter McGeachie are pictured presenting a silver candlestick to the Mayor of Reading, Councillor Doris Lawrence on the occasion of their Silver Jubilee in 1989. An identical candlestick had been presented to the Borough of Reading in 1973 to mark the firm's 10th anniversary.*

Pay RBH AUDIOLOGY APPEAL

Twelve Thousand Six Hundred and Seventy Six Pounds

£12,676-00

It was against this background that a merger between John Holt & Partners and Goss & Co. was proposed. The two firms had been fierce, but friendly competitors for years but sharing information would help each business identify its strengths and weaknesses and, with luck, eliminate the latter. Improved career prospects for staff would be just one advantage. The two companies would however remain separate entities though benefiting from 'back office' savings.

Jack Holt and Michael King had much in common; both were Reading born and bred and both had attended Reading School. They were both keen golfers, and both belonged to the same golf club at Calcot Park - and both were keen supporters of Reading Football Club.

Above: *Jack Holt and his staff present a cheque to Lord Roshill, on behalf of the Royal Berkshire Hospital Audiology Appeal, with the proceeds from a fun run the firm organised in 1989.*

When in October 1999 the firm of John Holt & Partners became part of the Goss Group Plc the enlarged Goss Group would become the largest independently owned Financial Advisers / Insurance Brokerage Group in the Thames Valley. The combined strength enhanced the value and service available to clients and made the group large enough to negotiate vigorously with the big institutions on behalf of clients - but still not too big to forget the importance of personal service.

Today the team of advisers at John Holt & Partners offers a total financial planning service for life. Whether this be the purchase of a first home, the planning for the increasing cost of university education, or planning pension and investment arrangements, the company has the experience and knowledge to help.

The firm of John Holt and Partners has more than 20,000 clients who place their trust and cash in their safe hands. The clients range from high net-worth

mortgage front each year it places loans totalling £20 million with a wide range of lenders.

Following the merger with Goss & Co. Jack Holt would remain chairman of the firm he had started 36 years earlier.

When Jack Holt founded the business he was just 25 years old and clients would often ask 'Is this your father's business?' By the end of the century clients were asking 'Are you still here?' How the years fly by, and who could have predicted back in the days when the Beatles were making their first appearances on 'Top of the Pops' that in the early years of the 21st century the name of John Holt would have come to be synonymous with sound financial advice throughout Reading and the Thames Valley. What has been the secret of achieving such a high reputation? It's no secret according to the firm: all one has to do is treat clients as if they were members of one's own family, and if a product is not good enough for an adviser's sister then it is not good enough for the firm's clients!

fifty-something investors, through young people setting up life assurance, mortgage and pension plans all the way to young children with savings plans earmarked for university fees.

On the investment side the firm has placed some £50 million in a variety of investments - cash accounts, ISAs, With profit Bonds and Unit Trusts.

The Pensions Department looks after regular annual contributions of more than £6 million and on the

Top left: Jack Holt and some of his staff, all ex pupils of Reading School, pose for the media in 1993.
Below: Michael King and Jack Holt following the merger between their companies in 1999.

Travel Incorporate

Travel Incorporate was acquired by the Goss group in 1991. The firm specialises in business travel, offering airline tickets, hotels, car rental, foreign currency, and visa facilities.

Used by many of Goss & Co.'s insurance clients as an extension of the company's services Travel Incorporate has a synergy with the group's other core businesses, its travel agency arm - Brooking - with offices from Wallingford to Reading.

Travel Incorporate was founded in 1987 in Pangbourne by entrepreneur and computer hardware dealer David Moore, who quickly built up the company to a good size through his connections with the IT industry.

By 1991 however with the economy going through a recession David decided to sell Travel Incorporate to the Goss Group. By then Goss had three retail travel agencies trading as Brooking Travel and decided to branch out into the business travel sector.

The company survived by finding new business and today's main clients are fast-growing corporations mainly in the hi-tech and communications industries.

Under its new ownership Travel Incorporate moved to Reading. Since then the company has expanded from just three people to fifteen and a turnover of £15 million. How? By returning all its commission to customers and charging a flat fee instead, the company has eliminated the normal conflict of interest between clients and the traditional travel agent.

The company's personal service is legendary: when a client's passport was lost in the post and he was due to travel at 9am the following day, a Travel Incorporate manager went to the Post Office at 4.30 am and spent an hour locating the 'Special Delivery' envelope; she then jumped in a cab and delivered the passport to the amazed client at 6.30 am outside his flat in London SW7 just ten minutes before his cab arrived to take him to Gatwick Airport.

It is rare to find a travel service provider which really will do whatever it takes to deliver an outstanding level of service.

Below: *Staff in the offices of Travel Incorporate.*

Brooking Travel

Travel agents have been around for a surprisingly long time. Not quite long enough to have organised the trip Chaucer's pilgrims made to Canterbury but still long ago enough to have established the idea that it makes sense to get someone else to do the hard work of booking hotels, planes, and coaches.

The first travel agents of modern times appeared with the railways. Block bookings for excursions to religious meetings started the ball rolling and there have been travel agents ever since. The British Government even used a firm of travel agents to ship troops to the Sudan to fight the Mad Mahdi and avenge the death of General Gordon at the battle of Omdurman. Anyone fancying a trip to Khartoum today might well ask the Reading firm of Brooking Travel for advice.

Brooking Travel was founded in 1981 as MWF Carter Ltd before being bought three years later by Alec Brooks and Michael King who commenced trading under the name of Brooking Travel.

Alec had previously managed the two Pickfords Travel shops in Reading (which later became Going Places) and Michael King was Managing Director of Goss & Co. Insurance Brokers.

At first, all business with tour operators was done by telephone, though it is now done by direct computer link.

A new shop in Reading's Market Place has state of the art communications based around the internet and industry software integrated using internet protocols

The business began from 42 Kings Road where the firm stayed for two years before moving to the Bristol and West Arcade opposite Marks and Spencer's side doors.

The biggest challenge faced by the firm was Marks and Spencer closing its side doors; this resulted in a dramatic reduction in passing trade.

That challenge was met by being different from other travel agents. Today the firm specialises in up-market and specialist holidays with a more individual touch for Reading folk who are looking for something unique or more unusual than a typical Spanish Costa holiday.

The firm now offers Reading the widest choice of holidays with over 600 different suppliers and a wealth of experience to back it up.

As well as booking their holidays staff like to see clients on other occasions. Each year Brooking takes its older clients on a free mystery coach tour and also hosts annual open days offering clients refreshments and an opportunity to have an informal chat with its experienced staff.

Both pictures: *Brooking Travel in the Bristol and West Arcade, offering a multitude of holiday destinations for the discerning traveller.*

'Rolling, rolling, rolling', as Frankie Laine once sang at the start of 'Rawhide', the popular TV show of 40 years ago, would have suited this herd making its way across Reading Bridge in 1923. Was that Gil Favor or Rowdy Yeats walking at the side, making sure that any strays were rounded up for branding? In truth, this mighty procession was testing out the resilience of the structure prior to the grand opening ceremony on 23 October 1923. It was a fine feat of engineering, but what a pity that the modern designers of London's millennium bridge could not have inherited similar skills. Their handiwork lasted but 24 hours before being closed on safety grounds as it bucked and swayed under the feet of those trying to use it. This bridge was part of Reading's major redevelopment programme that had been frustrated by the outbreak of war. Reading Bridge was constructed to meet the needs of the growing number of motor cars on the road and improvements to the river banks were also made. Flats and offices have now replaced the former surrounding industrial area of large chimneys and timber yards. The old steam rollers now appear as period pieces at country fairs, leaving us to our thoughts, inspired by this photograph, of 'head 'em up, move 'em out', as they used to call on the cattle drives across America.

On the move

Some brand names have been with us for a long time, part of the British way of life. Hovis conjures up memories of lads in flat caps, walking up a cobblestoned street with a basket full of fresh loaves. Typhoo has always been part of our tradition, providing that good old English cuppa, but the advert on the tram, recommending it as a cure for indigestion and suggesting it might be prescribed by the GP, 'ask your doctor', seems too much to swallow. Nufix was the equivalent of today's hair gel, used as an aid to grooming that has seen men experiment with Brilliantine and Brylcreem in the intervening years. The attraction of these products for the opposite sex always

did seem dubious, for which young lady really did want to run her fingers through a boyfriend's hair caked in grease? On board the tram one passenger seems to be getting something of a telling off, possibly for jumping on somewhere other than the designated stop. This Number 21 tram was photographed at the Cemetery Junction, an apt name for a terminus that would find its own graveyard on 20 May 1939 when the last passengers were carried. Trolley buses took over many of their routes on a service Reading Tramways Company had begun in 1879, though it had been taken over by Reading Corporation in 1901 as the condition of both the tramcars and the horses was giving cause for concern.

The trams along Oxford Road and Broad Street carried shoppers and workers to and from town almost until the start of the second world war. When the horse drawn trams were replaced by those running on the new electrified system on 21 July 1903, there was huge excitement as locals marvelled at one of the wonders of the modern age. It was a great period of development in transport for, as well as trams, motor cars were appearing on the streets and the Wright brothers were pioneering air travel at Kitty Hawk. The railways had opened up vast continents and ocean going liners had made the world seem a much

smaller place. At the Mill Lane depot the mayoress was given the honour of switching on the current that enabled the first electric tram to move along its tracks. The occasion was marked with lunch at the Town Hall and a large crowd cheered as the official opening ceremony was concluded. Looking at these trams in 1935 is a reminder that, although an efficient form of transport, many of their top decks were reserved for the hardy and well wrapped traveller. The open tops were exposed to the eccentricities of the English climate. Some models had open cabs where the driver sat, with no alternative for him but to brave the elements.

The traffic ground to a halt everywhere in the country on Coronation Day in 1953, not just in the square in front of the Town Hall. Britannia sat imperiously on her throne on the garlanded float, flanked by her attendants, in this splendid scene of pomp and pageantry. Queen Victoria gazed regally from her plinth upon the procession in honour of her great-great grand-daughter. Flags waved and bunting flew as we enjoyed our first national celebrations since VE and VJ Days. The rejoicing then was tinged with sadness for the ones who never made it back, but the investiture of a new monarch was a real occasion of unbridled joy. It was also the catalyst for the rapid growth in television ownership that took off later in the 1950s. The few who owned sets when Elizabeth II was being crowned suddenly found that they were amongst the most popular of neighbours. People to whom they had hardly done more than nod the odd greeting suddenly became bosom buddies as they crowded into the living room to look with wonder at the flickering black and white picture on the goggle box in the corner. Curtains were drawn, just like in the blackout era, as the richly reverberating tones of Britain's top commentator, Richard Dimbleby, described the scene in Westminster Abbey with appropriate dignity and solemnity. Then it was off into the street and let the party begin.

Below: During the second world war it was important to keep spirits high as the privations hit hard at home. By 1941 we had entered the grimmest period of the hostilities overseas and were facing major difficulties at home. Athens fell to the Germans as the British were pushed out of Greece, Yugoslavia buckled under the blitzkrieg in the Balkans, Rommel's Afrika Korps swept across the desert and our allies in Russia were faced with panzer divisions forcing them back from the Baltic Sea to the Black Sea. Nearer to home, London was still suffering from the almost nightly blitz from the skies and our own resources were running perilously low. Clothing was the latest item to require ration coupons to be tendered, as precious material was needed for uniforms for the armed forces. To boost morale, parades were held on our streets. Marching bands accompanied members of the services and civil defence workers as they defiantly lifted two fingers in a victory promise and a message to the little dictator. The tank displayed the war trophy a member of the Royal Berkshires had captured when the Norwegian Lofoten Islands were attacked in March 1941. It was a small, but morale boosting victory when, in a daring dawn raid on factories producing glycerine for explosives. To complete the good news, a power station, oil storage tanks and 11 German ships were also destroyed.

Above: In Elizabethan times London Street was a wide thoroughfare, containing many houses with impressive gardens. It was one of two main roads to the south of the Kennet and linked up with the main road to the capital, as its name implies. London Court is off here now, a collection of business units trying to look like canalside warehouses, but in 1960 the west side included a number of little shops, similar to the one at no 132. The hoardings and displays advertised a variety of cigarettes that had no restrictions upon how they extolled their relative attractions. The filter tipped Craven A even suggested that you smoke them 'for your throat's sake', a remarkable claim that would have lawyers rubbing their hands with glee today at the thought of the damages they could seek from such a statement. Whilst we can well do without Woodbines, known as 'coffin nails' even before health scares, it is good to see some of the other traditional names making a comeback. Tizer, 'the appetiser', is on the shelves again, with Vimto also nudging its way back into our consciousness. It can only be a matter of time before modern youth discovers the unique flavour of dandelion and burdock and the true taste of proper cream soda or old fashioned ginger beer.

ehind the van the sleek rear end of a Jaguar can be spotted, just as the Ford Anglia pulled away from the kerb in Market Place on a gloomy day in 1965. The cars were a contrast of the opulent and utilitarian lifestyles of their owners, but Reading has always been able to strike a balance between the two. Whatever the motorists standing in society each had respect for others around them, for road rage had yet to be invented. They also had a regard for the ears of pedestrians, not having windows wound down whilst the huge speakers of CD players blast out an unholy row that is supposed to be popular music. Has the more mature reader ever had the urge to pay these people back in kind, by driving up to a group of youths and letting rip with Eddie Cochran's 'C'mon everybody' or, better

still, really annoying them with Max Bygraves' 'Tulips from Amsterdam' at full volume? That last one would teach them a lesson. Sutton's Garden Shop was the most interesting establishment in Market Place at this time, having a history dating back to the beginning of the 19th century. In 1807, when John Sutton set up as a corn and seed merchant, his son Martin, a keen botanist, took great pains in making the seed beds and nurseries a success. Together they established the business that initially catered for local farmers coming to market, but expanded with the introduction of the penny post in 1840 to become nationally famous for its catalogues and mail order service. Sutton's left Reading for Torquay in 1976 because new road building had disrupted plans to extend its seed beds.

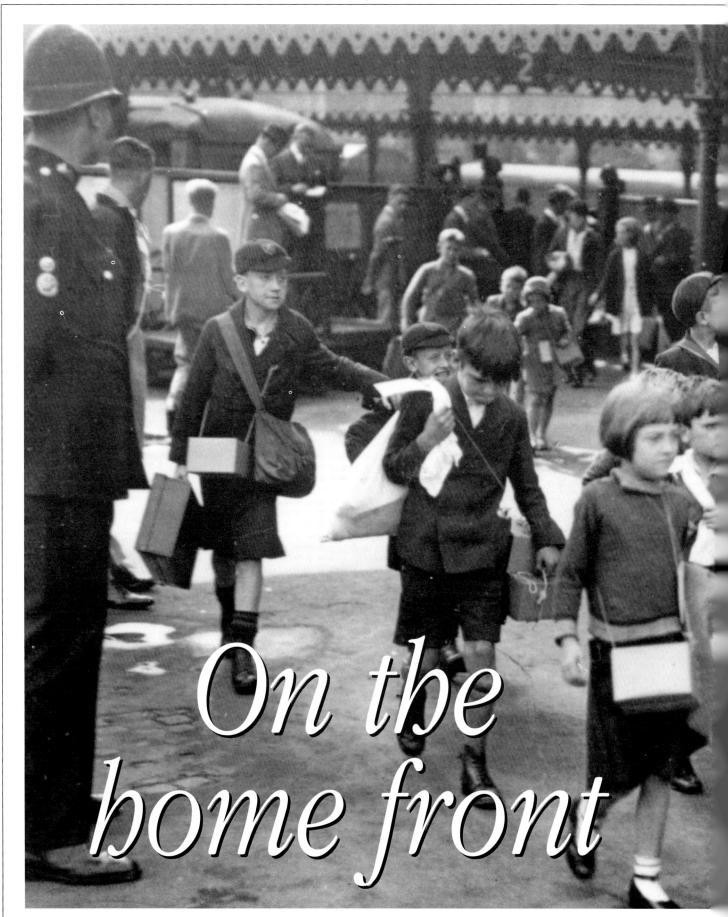

On the home front

Reading was declared a safe haven, one likely to escape the excesses of bombing, as Hitler's Panzer divisions began to roll across Europe. On 1 September 1939 the first wave of evacuees, mainly from London's East End, made its way through the doors of Reading station. They were to spend some restless nights at the United Reform Church in Broad Street before being moved to billets where householders were paid 10s 6d (52.5p) for giving a child a home. Many of the kiddies came on their own, leaving behind tearful mothers who had seen them off, just hoping that they would be all right. They came with a sense of bewilderment, names and destinations written on cards around their necks, to receive mixed welcomes. Some were happily received into host families, but others had more painful experiences. In one single house on East Street 17 children were packed into uncomfortable accommodation that left them red eyed and homesick. Of the 25,000 evacuees who came to Reading, half were children, the remainder being mainly mothers and invalids. Although some stayed for most of the war years, many returned home after a few months, during the period of the phoney war when little seemed to be happening. They would regret that decision when the blitz on London began in the autumn of 1940.

As the war years ground remorselessly by, more and more items came to be rationed. Hemlines rose as women eked out what material they had for dressmaking, finance and supply dictating fashion. In June 1943 the queues for new ration books, full of precious coupons, stretched a long way down Friar Street. What was not rationed was priced out of reach of the ordinary man in the street, so the system of limits being applied across the board was accepted as being the fairest way of dealing with shortages. At least the poorest members of society knew that the rich and powerful had to manage on a few ounces of bacon each week, just like everyone else. A free for all would have meant that money bought nourishment and poverty purchased starvation. The equality of treatment under rationing also helped foster a mood of togetherness that helped the country's class structure blur the boundaries and work with one another. A peer of the realm had to take a bath in five inches of water, just like a terraced house dweller, even if one had gold taps fitted and the other kept his on a peg in the back yard. Rationing was not just a passing phase, restricted to the war years. It continued long after hostilities ended as we struggled to get through the years of austerity that came in peacetime, not being completely phased out until 1954.

Although the town saw nowhere near the amount of carnage inflicted upon it that Coventry, Bath, Exeter and York saw, when the Luftwaffe did strike the effect was dramatic. On 10 October 1943 a lone Dornier DO217 came in low over Reading, dropping a stick of bombs that fell across the town centre from Minster Street to the corner of Friar Street. There was scant opportunity for the townspeople to be warned of the plane's approach as it strafed Caversham and north Reading before leaving this scene of devastation in its wake. St Laurence's Church lost most of its stained glass and its pinnacles were so badly damaged that they had to be taken down. The back of Wellsteed's store and part of Market Arcade were damaged, with the Town Hall taking an awful hammering. The saddest part of the tale was told in the People's Pantry, a restaurant crowded with people enjoying a meal at the end of the working day. A direct hit on the building killed 41, injuring even more. The cries of those trapped and the sight of mangled limbs stayed forever in the memories of rescue workers as they risked their own lives, scrambling through the rubble in a valiant effort to reach the victims. Wartime days were not times of jolly togetherness, but of deprivation, pain, fear and tragedy.

Above: Workmen picked their way carefully through the rubble of what had been the pride and joy of families for whom these had been more than houses. They were their homes, lovingly cherished places where children had been brought into the world, personalised by ornaments and photographs on the mantelpiece. These had all been smashed to smithereens on 27 November 1940 when Cardiff Road was hit in a bombing raid. It was not so much the loss of bricks and mortar that hurt, but the destruction of so many keepsakes and the memories they held. That picture of the little one's christening, granddad's war medals and the souvenirs of seaside holidays disappeared in the dust and flames that wrecked the buildings. The bombs were intended for the nearby rail yards and signal box, but a small error in aiming cost Cardiff Road dear. People living elsewhere only knew of the raid and the havoc it wreaked by word of mouth, because press censorship meant that it was reported simply as 'considerable damage to working class properties in a home counties town'. That did not tell the half of it, of lives lost and futures ruined. But, as the slogans reminded us, 'Careless talk costs lives' and 'Be like dad, keep mum'. It was only after the war that the full extent of the bombing campaigns on our homeland became widely known.

Below: This poor little mite could have been dressed for her first taste of space travel, but this was no helmet for some future traveller in an Apollo mission. She was trying out one of a consignment of baby's gas masks that had arrived in town in August 1939. Civil defence exercises were frequent as we waited for the inevitable news that we were to be at war. Responses to air raids were practised, dummy evacuations took place and measures to counter gas attacks were taken. The fear of chemical and even biological warfare was very real, as many soldiers from the first world war recounted their experiences at Ypres when chlorine gas was used with devastating effect. Mustard gas was another weapon used by both sides, though the poison gas was difficult to control as changes in wind direction sometimes led to troops being injured by their own side's weapons. In 1939, with the real threat that gas shells could be dropped from the air with no risk to the attacker, Britain viewed the situation very seriously. Mums collected masks for the family from central points and anxiously practised their use. Fortunately, so great was the fear of reprisal attack, neither side made use of chemical weapons and gas masks were happily consigned to the attic and a place on the history shelf.

Getting spruced up for Christmas these little ones are on their way back home. Some had been evacuated earlier in the war, whilst others had been born some distance from the capital city in which their parents had grown up. By late November 1944 the Allies had captured Aachen, the first German city to fall, and troops were advancing on Cologne and across the Saarland. The waves of V-2 rockets had stopped and it seemed safe to return to London. These children had been in Wales and were making an overnight stop at Katesgrove School, where they were thoroughly scrubbed before setting off on the final leg of their journey. Katesgrove does not owe its name to the diminutive of some ancient Catherine who might have lived in the area, but to the herds of cattle or 'cattes' who once grazed there. The district claimed to have played a part in Nelson's victory at Trafalgar, in 1805, as naval sailcloth was produced in large volumes in Katesgrove. The children and their mothers were not too interested in tales of the sea, being more interested in seeing their homes once again. They sang 'Mairzy Doats' and other daft ditties that echoed the happy way they felt, but would have been saddened if they had realised that the popular bandleader, Glenn Miller, only had a month left to live. The American trombonist, who gave the world 'In the Mood' and 'Moonlight Serenade', went missing on a flight across the Channel.

'This country is now at war with Germany,' were the fateful words spoken by Prime Minister Neville Chamberlain that came crackling down the radio waves into our living rooms on 3 September 1939 as we arrived home from church ready to prepare the Sunday lunch. It was a bright, sunny day as the children in Palmer Park enjoyed the last slide of peace that they would experience for nearly six years. By the time the armistice was signed some of these youngsters would have outgrown such youthful pursuits, having lost their childhood to a time of shortages, fear and sadness. They could not play happily on the swings and roundabouts without keeping an ear cocked for the sound of the air raid siren that would send them rushing to the nearest Anderson shelter. Eventually, many of their playgrounds and open spaces would disappear as climbing frames and their like were dismantled for scrap or dug over as allotments. Parents did not like to let children out of their sight, in case they became separated should an attack be launched. That anxiety meant that normal relaxed family life was put under a strain from which some did not recover. When some young people went off the rails in the 1950s they blamed, in part, their unsettled upbringing during that period of our history when childhood was suspended. Not all the casualties of war were to be found on the battlefield or in the bombed out ruins at home.

Shopping spree

Looking from the south along St Mary's Butts in 1935, with Holmes' new store on the left, brings back to mind an age when the motor car did not dominate the streets. Pedestrians could amble at their own pace across the wide expanse of carriageway without having to run for their lives. It is possible that the young women had just left Powell's and were examining the holiday snaps that had been developed from the roll of film left there the week before. A little box Brownie provided people with just as much pleasure as a digital camera with a zoom lens or some multi function camcorder that had virtually instant playback. There is something satisfying about waiting for the prints to be developed, anticipation being as much fun as the actual event. Let us hope they did not get too engrossed in their photos because, although the roads were quiet, there were still dangers about for the unwary. Despite the smaller volume of traffic, accidents were too frequent for anyone's liking. Safety measures came in by the bucket load, with a driving test for all new drivers and pedestrian crossings being introduced in 1934. In the following year the 30 mph speed limit was imposed in built up areas and Percy Shaw's cat's eyes were added to the white lines on roads that had only been painted there since 1926.

Like some fairy tale castle that would not be out of place on a mountain top in Ruritania, McIlroy's department and grocery store was amongst the créme de la créme of shopping. Its sweeping frontage on the north side of Oxford Road, the glorious architecture of its gables, cornices and turrets and the huge amount of 'crystal palace' glass on the first floor marked it as something special. That was even before you stepped inside to be greeted by a grandeur that made shopping here an opulent experience. The store opened in 1903 at a time when Edwardian ladies, in their crinolines and gowns, were making shopping a personal and social experience. In more prim Victorian times they waited in their carriages whilst servants made purchases on their behalf, but the new age and the rising tide of feminism brought them inside the doors. One daring young thing can even be seen approaching McIlroy's on a bicycle - what courage, what panache, what brazenness! After the second world war individual department stores felt the pinch from the big boys in charge of High Street chain stores, as Heelas was taken over by United Drapery in 1949 and by John Lewis in 1953, the same year as Bull's closed. Wellsteed's eventually came under Debenham's wing, but by then mighty McIlroy's had served its last customer, ringing up the last tills in 1955. The building remains, though without many of its attractive ornamental features.

est Street, linking Friar Street and Broad Street, is now one of those subject to 'pedestrian hours', when, for most of the shopping day, vehicles are banned from the town centre. No such problems faced locals in 1935 as trams, vans and cars merrily buzzed along towards the junction with St Mary's Butts, in the distance to the south. At No 27, David Greig's grocery and butcher's store was popular with shoppers as it catered for a variety of purchases for the larder. In the days before the thought police of the health and safety divisions or the food standards authorities moved in, there was game and poultry hanging on huge

hooks outside the shop, giant cheeses within waited to be sliced and assistants greeted their customers like old friends. A cheery, 'How's the bronchial tubes today, missus, do they need a touch of massage?' would provoke either a witty response or a severe bout of coughing. The pungent aroma of cured hams, intermingling with evocative farmyard smells on new laid eggs, started mouths slavering on entering the shop. Housewives proffered shillings, pence and farthings to the man behind the counter. He had weighed it all in pounds and ounces without worrying about being hauled up before the beak for failing to use some foreign measurement foisted upon him.

Above: Looking east along Friar Street, from the Station Road junction, we can see the Town Hall in the distance. Once known as New Street, it owes its name to the friars of St Francis of Assisi who built their church here in 1311. Greyfriars Church was restored and reconsecrated as an Anglican church in 1863. Behind the camera, Friar's Walk shopping centre opened in 1974, by which time Sainsbury's was already well established on Friar Street, having arrived in 1963, marking the beginning of the end for many of the small shops as the day of the supermarket arrived. In the 1990s the street began to acquire a notoriety associated with the noisy bars and new style pubs that opened, most of them sporting daft names to do with toads, newts and rats. Perhaps some of these descriptions are appropriate, after all, but in 1930 it was a more genteel place to promenade on a Friday evening. Part of the quieter life seen in those days could be linked to the lack of money in people's pockets, for the country was in the grips of a depression. Unemployment was high and belts were tightened as we faced the prospect of not enough food on our plates to feed every hungry mouth. Little surprise, then, that we had little to spend in the Boar's Head.

What a busy scene on Broad Street as pedestrians and motorists mixed on the carriageway, each dodging the other. It has been over 30 years since this was possible, as all but essential traffic was excluded from here in 1970, followed by full pedestrianisation in the early 1990s. Surprisingly, the picture dates from 1945 when petrol restrictions still bit hard, but the number of vehicles suggests that perhaps a few gallons of precious fuel had become available to help celebrate the end of the war. Marks and Spencer, on the right, is still a familiar sight on Broad Street, but Timothy Whites and Taylors, once a great rival of Boots, has gone to that great prescription in the sky.

Reading's main shopping area was closed to most traffic just after the first section of the inner distribution road was opened. Formerly the site of the sheep market, within its width Broad Street was once held a collection of several streets that included Butcher Row, Cheese Row and Fish Row. The lovely prism shaped terracotta roof of the building on the corner of Queen Victoria Street is a delightful example of the use of bricks and tiles produced locally at Katesgrove and Tilehurst. The council had the good sense to incorporate this aspect of the town's history into the pedestrianised Broad Street, creating a more colourful and charming effect than the plain flagging introduced by other towns.

The car and van below the hoarding have a lovely period feel, with their tiny wing-mounted sidelights, protruding headlights, external spare wheels and running boards. They could be straight from an episode of the 'Untouchables', with Eliot Ness fighting off Al Capone's mobsters as they machine gunned their way across Chicago. In reality, bargains galore were available at Holmes' store on the west side of St Mary's Butts in 1932 and Reading shoppers were not slow to take advantage. There was a road widening scheme about to be put into action and some of the buildings had to go in the name of progress, a much used excuse down several generations as many examples of our heritage were bulldozed into oblivion. Holmes and Son got a shiny new store out of the redevelopment process, but not everyone was so fortunate. St Mary's Butts was the heart of the old town from where the housing expansion along the London and Southampton roads began, as long ago as the 13th century. Archers practised their craft in this vicinity, hence the name of the road. The only use for their arrows these days would be as pointed sticks with which to stab and pick up the litter that picnickers leave strewn all over the grass in front of St Mary's every sunny lunchtime.

Above: This view of the east side of St Mary's Butts in the late 1960s is an apt reminder of the changing shopping patterns that were emerging. Baylis had been a straightforward family grocer, but had to adapt to consumer demands, becoming a supermarket. For many businesses it was the beginning of the end of personal service and speciality shops. You could not conduct a friendly conversation with a valued customer or inquire about her hubby's health whilst weighing out a pound of best back bacon when it is all prepacked and presented at the checkout with the other purchases. Shoppers started to demand that everything be found under one roof and, before long, the giant supermarkets and shopping malls were upon us. Even supermarkets like Baylis's found it difficult to compete with the pile 'em high, sell 'em cheap brigade as a stranglehold was put on smaller outlets. Underneath the trolley bus wires, another relic of the period, a little invalid carriage was making its tentative way along the road. These flimsy contraptions offered poor protection in the event of a collision and it always seemed unfair that the vulnerable in our society had to be put in danger for the sake of some freedom of mobility.

St Laurence's, the town's municipal church, stood overlooking Market Place in the early summer of 1941 as a remarkable scene unfolded in front of it. In 1539 a crowd gathered to witness the hanging, drawing and quartering of Hugh Faringdon a few hundred yards away from Market Place, at the west front of the Abbey, he was the last Abbot of Reading. He met his grisly fate for failing to acknowledge Henry VIII as head of the Church, but it was a more modest attraction that brought people into Market Place four centuries later. The humble orange was the centre of interest as word spread that supplies of the fruit had arrived on the stalls. Once commonplace commodities became rarities in the shops as imports dried up with merchant ships unable to bypass the ring of steel that enemy submarines had thrown around our shores. Those who grew up in the war will be able to remember the thrill of seeing their first banana, starved as they were of such exotic experiences in a diet restricted by rationing and shortages. Carrots replaced dried fruit in Christmas puddings and Lord Woolton, the Minister of Food, recommended his revolting pie of turnips, swedes and parsnips as an alternative to steak and kidney. Was it any wonder that hundreds queued, just for the chance of tasting one juicy orange? Most of them did so in vain, but vowed to get up earlier if there was to be a next time.

At work

In the first world war women played important roles, especially as nurses, drivers and factory workers who took over jobs vacated by men who had enlisted to fight the enemy. This inspired many more, escaping from the yoke of traditional male dominance, to flex their muscles in the workplace during the years between the wars. As the storm clouds settled over Europe again in the late 1930s, women stepped forward from the shadows once more, this time in even greater numbers and into more obviously identifiable positions in civil defence and the later war effort. Seen in July 1939 at Brock Barracks, these are some of the members of the Auxiliary Territorial Service (ATS) checking stores before the balloon finally went up at the beginning of September. There were still deeply held beliefs in some quarters, including government, that women should just render first aid, provide food or operate telephones during times of conflict, but hundreds of thousands ignored prejudice and mobilised. The ATS was formed in 1938, following in the wake of the Women's Army Auxiliary Corps founded in 1917. They wore khaki uniforms, like their male counterparts, but struggled to play a full part in the first two years of the war, frustrated by such Winston Churchill decrees that they should not fire anti aircraft guns in case they were upset by the knowledge that they had killed a young German airman. Although still banned from pulling the metaphorical trigger, they were eventually permitted to track planes, fuse shells and be present when they were fired. Over 200,000 joined the ATS and the organisation was not disbanded until 1949, when it was absorbed into the Women's Royal Army Corps.

Is your old granny in her 90s and has she always grumbled about silly girls who swoon over film stars and moon about pretty boy pop icons? Could she never understand why we screamed when those four mopheads from Liverpool sang 'Twist and shout', why our kids went around in tartan, yelling, 'We love the Rollers' or that youngsters today fall over themselves to catch a glimpse of the lads from Westlife? If the cap fits, then find her on this picture of the workforce at Huntley and Palmer's on 26 June 1926, when not a single female was on the factory floor, but hanging out of the windows to get a better view of the parade along Kings Road. It was not some forerunner of James Dean that was causing hearts to flutter, but the most eligible bachelor in Britain was passing by underneath. Edward, Prince of Wales was the man stirring the girls to flights of fancy as he acknowledged their squeals of delight with a jaunty wave that drove each one of those watching to a frenzy in the belief that the recognition was just for her. His royal visit to Reading was the high spot of the year and every impressionable girl cuddled her pillow a little tighter that night in the secure knowledge that she had caught his eye. Now then, gran, what was that you were saying about Leonardo di Caprio?

Below: A recruitment meeting for the Women's Land Army (WLA) was being advertised outside that organisation's headquarters in Market Place in April 1940. It had the added attraction of an organ recital, in an effort to swell the numbers attending, hardly needed by Reading women who volunteered their services without the need for such inducements. Local girls mixed with those who came from London to do their bit for the war effort, being paid the princely sum of one shilling (5p) an hour, but having to pay 28s (£1.40) per week board and lodging if they were billeted with a family or on a farm. It was hardly profitable work from a financial standpoint, but the benefits to the country could not be measured in pounds, shillings and pence. The Land Army girls kept food production going, for without them there would not have been enough hands to till the soil, drive the tractors, care for the livestock and get in the crops. The WLA, first called into action during the Great War, was reformed n 1939. Only 7,000 joined during the first year of the war, so recruitment drives, like this one, were held across Britain. The government tried to glamourise the work in its adverts, but the reality was much different. The work was tough and young women usually worked in isolated communities, often in old farm cottages without running water, gas or electricity.

Right: Air raid shelters, in their various guises, appeared on the streets of every town, in back gardens and in open fields across the country. Outside JM Stone's lighting specialists, this one in Market Place, being given its finishing touches in October 1939, was amongst 40 that were erected in Reading town centre during the war. Government advice on their use varied between the practical and the ludicrous. Useful drills were held, usually organised by civil defence groups, whereby people became used to responding to air raid warning sirens and were ready to take to the shelters at a moment's notice. They had emergency bags packed and provisions laid in for use in private shelters, but regarded some of the official advice as quaint, to say the least. One authoritative leaflet offered particular advice to women, as if they had no minds of their own. It suggested they should have tailored slacks and a warm, woolly jumper to hand in case of a night-time attack, as bedtime lingerie would be unsuitable attire. Whether this was because a nightie would be too cold or too provocative was never addressed by the powers that be! Fortunately, Reading escaped the greatest excesses of the wartime bombing raids, but it was reassuring to know that there were some havens to reach when the drone of the Heinkels, Junkers and Dorniers were heard in the skies above.

Below: Part of Bull's drapery store in Broad Street was reserved as a waste paper exhibition area, encouraging visitors to save valuable paper and donate old magazines, books and catalogues that could be recycled for such different uses as packaging or fuel briquettes. Salvage targets were regularly set for towns and, during this drive, Reading was asked to achieve the equivalent of a cargo ship full of paper by the end of the year. The response was typical of the spirit that spurred us on to ensure that seemingly impossible targets were not only met, but eclipsed. After just two weeks of collecting Reading's waste paper salvage stocks yielded an impressive 177 tons. Much of the credit given for the success of such efforts can be directed towards the fact that we are an island race. Geographically, we are isolated from the rest of Europe, giving us the reputation of being stand offish and somewhat aloof. During the war those characteristics came to our aid, as we found ourselves on our own when France, Belgium and the others went under. There was no one else to turn to, until America came into the war, and the British pulled together in the common cause. United behind an inspirational prime minister, the nation applauded Winston Churchill when he declared, 'Men will say, this was their finest hour'.

Bottom right: GR Jackson's scrap iron depot on Chatham Street was working around the clock, collecting countless lorry loads of aluminium and other metals in August 1940. Piled high with precious scrap, their cargoes would be transformed into new fighting machines in a matter of weeks. The nation rallied to the cause, fuelled by a fervour that made people become besotted with salvage and fundraising. It was not just metal that was collected, there were mountains of paper and books waiting to be recycled. Bones were collected for reprocessing as cordite for shells, fertiliser and animal feed. Material and rags were bundled and set on to reappear as parachutes, blankets and uniforms. Every other week there seemed to be a

drive for money as warship week came, Hurricane week went and tank week followed. Towns competed with each other in national league tables to see which could be the most generous, with thermometers appearing on town halls and churches, charting the amounts of cash donated. In Russia Week, in February 1942, Reading helped the rest of the country to raise over £1.3 million to help provide a warship for our allies. Although not funded by such means, one of our navy's own warships proudly bore the town's name. The HMS Reading, formerly an American destroyer, accompanied the battleship that carried Winston Churchill across the Atlantic from his important meeting with President Roosevelt in 1941.

Far right: Even as early in the war as July 1940, it was realised that our resources were going to be stretched to breaking point. We stood alone as U-boats circled our shores, cutting off supplies from abroad. We needed aeroplanes, tanks and ships to fight the enemy and so much equipment had been left behind in France when the British Expeditionary Force was driven back across the Channel. Operation Dynamo, the great evacuation of Dunkirk in June 1940, was a wonderfully gallant and successful exercise in getting our boys home. The joy of rescuing so many was good propaganda, but the truth was that we had suffered a heavy defeat and lost a lot

of our firepower. The word went out for scrap metal to be collected and for sacrifices to be made in the name of the war effort. This aluminium collecting centre in a shopping arcade took in pots, pans, bedwarmers and anything that could be melted down and recycled into a Spitfire or other machine that would be sent into service in the defence of our country. There was a huge collection point at the railway yards as people rallied to the cause, donating other metals as they tore down fences, gates and railings. Salvage became an obsession as nothing was discarded, but hoarded away ready for the next drive towards a new battleship to liberate the seas.

By January 1947 people began to ask one another who had really won the war, as the immediate postwar years were austere times. Rationing and shortages were still with us and the Labour government seemed to be trying to nationalise every major industry, despite Tory warnings that state monopoly was just a racket at the consumer's expense. The weekly meat ration was cut by nearly 15 per cent, bread was in short supply and bacon, fish and eggs all remained tightly controlled. As the new year dawned, the National Coal Board was born amidst lingering resentment in the coalfields, suggesting that Manny Shinwell, the Minister of Fuel, was in for a rocky ride. It all coincided with a hard winter of freezing tempera-tures and heavy snowfalls and conditions were made worse by a severe coal shortage. Many businesses worked shorter hours as electricity was restricted and shops resorted to candle power to illuminate their shelves. The men checking their change and purchases at Boots' counter would have done well to buy a stock of aspirin from the famous chemist's store, for there were further headaches to come that winter. In February the RAF had to drop supplies for stranded villagers in Norfolk, Lincolnshire and Yorkshire and food stocks were stretched all the more by the weather, as fishing fleets were kept in port and air travel thrown into chaos by the storms. We might have won the war, but winning the peace was becoming as big a problem.

Below: After the first world war we tried to rebuild and fulfil the pledge that there would be a land fit for heroes. We failed, as the dark days of the depression and the horrors of the second world war came upon us. So, we tried again as Reading Corporation started its first permanent housing programme in April 1946. Workmen, who had dug gardens and parks for victory in the war, now turned the sods for the future. Footings were dug, foundations laid and the piles of bricks were in place, waiting to be transformed into modern living units. At the time many of the older properties were little better than slums and 3,750 families had no home that they could call their own. As the town was badly overcrowded, new estates began to spring up on the empty land on the outskirts of Reading. The Whitley estate, begun before the war, was extended and, by the 1950s, new developments included Southcote, St Michael's, Meadway and Emmer Green. Conservationists went mad, bemoaning the loss of the countryside to the urban sprawl, but to no avail. Families were not to be denied the comforts of modern life, many of them having their own bathrooms for the first time. The days of the outdoor privy and bathnight in front of the living room fire were consigned to the memory banks.

The bottling plant at H and G Simonds' brewery was working flat out in the autumn of 1947, putting the finishing touches to a special royal brew. In a few weeks' time the foaming ale would be poured into glasses raised in honour of the marriage of Princess Elizabeth, daughter of George VI and heir to the throne, to Lieutenant Philip Mountbatten, the future Duke of Edinburgh. Their wedding took place on 20 November 1947 when, dressed in a gorgeous ivory bridal gown designed by Norman Hartnell, the 21 year old princess said 'I do' to the man who was destined to walk one step behind her into the next millennium. Many a drop of Simonds was drunk in recognition of the day. Younger readers might be amazed to learn that there used to be a time when we tipped beer from a bottle into a glass, rather than swigging it straight from the container whilst pressing a mobile phone to one ear. We had funny habits in the old days! Simonds' brewery was a Reading landmark for two centuries, dating back to its founding on Broad Street in 1785 by William Blackall Simonds. He moved production to Bridge Street in 1789, quickly establishing it as the largest in Reading. One of the family members, George Blackall Simonds, gained fame outside the business, being responsible for sculpting several of the town's monuments. His most notable work is the 1886 Maiwand Lion in Forbury Gardens. The brewery was taken over by Courage in 1960 and production in Bridge Street ceased in 1980.

Achieving success in a caring environment

The Abbey School was founded in 1887 as an independent school for girls. It moved to its present site in 1905. It is situated close to Reading town centre and railway station and enjoys good transport links by train and public buses.

The Abbey School grew out of a school started in 1887 when Blenheim House, a small private establishment run by a Miss Buckland and her two younger sisters, was taken over by the Church Schools' Company and became known as Reading High School. As the school has a Church of England foundation, the religious education syllabus and school assembly reflect this. Nevertheless, girls from all faiths or of none are welcome at the school and there is a diversity of ethnic backgrounds amongst the pupils.

One of the school's past Headmistresses had a reputation for being, 'an alarming disciplinarian, frequently reducing her pupils to tears'. Girls played hockey and tennis and took part in play productions. Games lessons were given in Palmer Park. Swimming lessons took place at 6.30 am in South Street Baths, and gymnastics classes were held at Reading School by an army sergeant at 7 pm. Later a gymnasium was fitted up (1899) and two classes were held each week. Netball did not become a school game until 1908.

In those days Reading had trams but there were no country buses. The school had a horse-drawn covered wagon, known as the school bus, which toured the town each morning and afternoon to collect and take home girls who did not live near the tram route. Girls living near Twyford used to walk to school. In 1902 records show that there were 32 pupils at the school.

The present site was bought at that time and plans were prepared for a school to hold 250 pupils. The expected aid from government legislation was not forthcoming, however and the building was reduced to provide accommodation for the teaching of 150 only.

Above left: Miss Musson MA, JP, Headmistress 1902 - 1935. Below: The original Abbey School pictured at the time when Jane Austen was a pupil.

Work began in the new building in 1905 with 79 girls in the school. The numbers did not grow very rapidly at first and each year a considerable amount of money had to be found to balance the accounts. They had to consider whether they would offer the building to Reading Borough Council but the school had good friends like Canon W M G Ducat and Sir John Carrington. They gathered a body of people together to form a committee which for five years gave time and money to save the school. At one time the position was so hopeless that the staff were given a provisional term's notice.

In 1913 it was decided to form a company to acquire the school (Now to be called The Abbey School) from the Church Schools' Company which gave them a favourable lease of the buildings with an option to buy as soon as possible. The collection of a fund was started for this purpose but less than £2000 had been subscribed when the First World War broke out and all private needs had to give way to the national necessity. Boarding houses were gradually introduced. Information taken from a leaflet giving

Top: The Common Room in the Sixth Form Centre in the early 1970s. **Above right:** *The Dean of St Paul's, the Very Revd. Martin Sullivan, MA, presenting awards at the Commemoration Service in 1974.*

particulars of the routine of the boarders makes interesting reading:
'Each girl has her own cubicle. French is spoken until after supper under the supervision of the resident French Governess. No Exeats, except during the half-term holiday, are in general allowed during term time, but girls may visit their friends on Saturday or Sunday afternoons at the request of their parents or guardians if an escort is provided for them both in going from and returning to the boarding house. Meals: 8 am Breakfast: Porridge, meat or fish with fruit, jam, marmalade, etc. 11 am Lunch: milk and biscuits. 1.30 pm Dinner: Meat, vegetables and pudding. 4 pm Tea. 6.45 pm supper: With eggs or fish, soup, pudding etc.

Fees were 23 guineas for full board per term, with an extra $2^1/_2$ guineas for laundry. Over the years the number of boarding pupils decreased and boarding was eventually discontinued.

The increase in numbers of day girls, however, became more rapid and the school began to pay its way.

Over recent years the school has been considerably extended, modernised and re-equipped to meet the educational requirements of the present day. The School has a tradition of outstanding academic achievement and has built a reputation of excellence in many spheres. Girls are encouraged to work hard to identify their own particular talents and all skills and achievements are celebrated. The school provides a varied general education, to enable each girl to develop her abilities fully. Each girl is encouraged to study widely and to be receptive to new ideas.

The many activities on offer in the Senior Department include a variety of Musical opportunities, Drama, many sports, the Duke of Edinburgh's Award and the Young Enterprise Scheme.

The school is divided into a Senior Department, in Kendrick Road and Junior and Preparatory Departments nearby in Christchurch Road. The school is organised and controlled as one complete unit. There are about 700 girls in the 11-18 range, including 160 in the Sixth Form. The latter have their own Sixth Form Centre, including common rooms, on site. The Junior and Preparatory Departments cater for about 250 girls from 4-9 years. Year six girls (ten year olds) are based in a separate building on the senior school site for

their transition year, where they are taught by Senior Department specialist staff, which eases the move from Junior to Senior School life.

The school has produced many women who have distinguished themselves in a wide variety of fields. Perhaps of special interest are the following as readers may well recognise them from their appearances in the local and national press. Minette Walters, the best-selling crime novelist is one such old girl, as is Gillian Reynolds an Arts Columnist for a national broadsheet newspaper. The acclaimed novelist, Elizabeth Taylor, whose novel Angel (1957) is set in the streets of Reading also attended the school. Anne Burns who held many women's world records as a glider pilot and became an air accident investigator, demonstrates that The Abbey is not confined to turning out famous women of letters.

Above left: *The new wing pictured in the late 1960s.*
Below left: *Miss B C L Sheldon, the School's current headmistress.* ***Below:*** *Junior School girls relaxing in the school's grounds.*

Going, going...

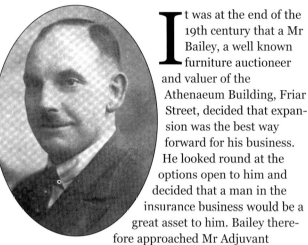

It was at the end of the 19th century that a Mr Bailey, a well known furniture auctioneer and valuer of the Athenaeum Building, Friar Street, decided that expansion was the best way forward for his business. He looked round at the options open to him and decided that a man in the insurance business would be a great asset to him. Bailey therefore approached Mr Adjuvant Cadence Thimbleby who at the time was working from 47 Queens Road as an insurance agent. Thimbleby agreed terms and the new firm of Bailey & Thimbleby was formally announced to the waiting world in the Reading Mercury of 18th May 1901.

This was the beginning of the firm known today as Thimbleby & Shorland, the famous Reading-based chartered surveyors, auctioneers, valuers and estate agents now located at 31 Great Knollys Street.

Those early days were spent in arranging auction sales of furniture in rooms beneath the Athenaeum Building, a sale room last used by WE Scotchbrook in the 1970s and since then converted into offices.

Messrs Bailey and Thimbleby were astute men and realised that Reading was a growing centre for agriculture. They agreed that to succeed they must be involved in auction sales in the rapidly growing Reading Cattle Market. They therefore approached George Shorland, a well respected farmer who was then farming at Sheephouse and Bolney Farms between Reading and Henley on Thames.

George Shorland agreed to run the agricultural side of the business and in the Reading Mercury of 27th October 1901 it was announced 'Messrs Bailey and Thimbleby have arranged to carry on the agricultural side of the business in conjunction with Mr George Shorland under the name and style of Messrs Bailey, Thimbleby & Shorland'.

Above left: *Lumley Thimbleby, son of the founder.*
Below: *Judging Shorthorn cattle in the street as the market was flooded in 1947.*

This new joint venture started the firm we know today. At that time auction sales in Reading Cattle market were already being conducted by Jenkins, Davies & Sons; Cottrell, Simmons & Goodchild; W Campins and Messrs Raynbird & Sons - but there has always been room at the top.

In January 1902 Messrs Bailey, Thimbleby & Shorland were advertising sales by auction in the Cattle Market of store stock and poultry; sales of household appointments, pianoforte and china however were still held under the banner of Bailey & Thimbleby - Shorland was not involved in that side of the business. Bailey & Thimbleby were also still selling property by private treaty and by auction from their Friar Street address.

And Adjuvant Cadence Thimbleby was not only still operating on his own as an insurance agent from 47 Queens Road but he was also advertising his insurance business as being based in the Cattle Market too.

Soon however Mr Bailey ceased to be involved with the firm, and all the adverts in the local press from 1903 onwards mention only the name of Thimbleby & Shorland.

The firm continued its expansion in the agricultural business and by 1911 Thimbleby & Shorland were selling store cattle on Saturdays, fatstock on Mondays whilst on Tuesdays they were operating at Wokingham Market as well.

Amongst the interesting sales in that first decade for the firm was one on 28th April 1911 on the instruction of the executors of one GD Lucas; the lots included three complete sets of road rollers including living vans, water carts and notice boards - and an eight horse-power traction engine. The sale of contractors plant would one day, still far in the future, eventually become a speciality of the firm.

Top: A cattle sale in 1925 with AC Thimbleby, in top hat, as auctioneer. Above: A Farmers' Desk Book presented to clients by the firm.

Thimbleby & Shorland had by now moved offices to Arcade Chambers in Station Road. The firm also took offices at 22 1/2 Bridge Street in Banbury so that sales could be conducted in the Banbury Cattle Market.

By the end of the Great war in 1918 Thimbleby & Shorland had become a nationally known firm of auctioneers selling livestock all over the country.

The period during the wars saw a great revival in the value of pedigree stock. The firm spent a lot of time conducting sales for various Milk Recording Societies throughout the country. Farmers were waking up to the idea that they must have the best milkers to obtain the greatest benefit for their efforts: there were sales advertised of Grand Coloury Dairy Shorthorns with recorded milk yields of between 7,000 and 12,000 lbs of milk a year per cow.

The first Autumn Show and Sale for the Oxon, Berks and Hants Milk Recording Societies was held at Reading on 30th September 1918. All entries averaged 750 gallons of milk per annum and a number had passed the tuberculin test as well! The advert said 'Do not Fail to attend' and just to make sure it added that luncheon would be served at the place of sale.

*Top: A flooded sale room in 1948. **Above:** A disgruntled bull being led to market through the flood waters.*

In April 1920 the firm held the first annual sale of '65 Exceptionally Choice well Bred Recorded Dairy Cattle' at Bristol Cattle market. There was prize money of £50 on offer. In the same month the first annual sale of Recorded Dairy Cattle was held at Leicester for the Derby, Melton Mowbray, Nottingham & Peak Milk Recording Societies. That sale included the First Prize winner from the London Dairy Show's Milking Trials. The sale averages for the

Bristol event was £64 11s 0d a head with a top price of 120 guineas paid by Lieutenant Colonel Holford for 'Mr Hawe's Mary'.

Even though Thimbleby & Shorland were selling dairy cattle all over the country one of the busiest departments was still the horse auctions. In 1918 after the end of the first world war His Majesty's Secretary of State for War had instructed the firm to sell army horses repatriated from France. The sales included heavy draught horses, vanners and cobs, with good prices achieved - the best 'heavies' making £96 12 s 0d, vanners £52 10s and cobs making £30.

By the first months of 1919 sales of army horses were being held weekly at Banbury, Oxford and Reading with AC Thimbleby, on 30th January, disposing of fifty horses in quick time at excellent prices.

Adverts in local papers praised these retired war horses:

> *Tried and passed the test*
> *They did their very best*
> *They worked to win the war*
> *They'll work for you still more.*

A fitting tribute to those excellent animals which had endured tough times in Flanders and elsewhere during the hostilities. Another advert of the time read 'Why buy expensive motors when there are good working horses to buy?' And at the time most would have agreed with those sentiments.

Throughout the 1920s agricultural sales continued to be the mainstay of the firm. In 1922 a Berkshire Boar pig famously fetched 400 guineas, an enormous sum at the time. But it would be volume rather than such unique prices which made the firm's name.

In 1924 one John Kirkwood who worked for the Country Gentlemen's Association was experiencing difficulty in getting cattle sold in Ireland; he arranged for a trainload to go to Reading from Waterford in Ireland.

Thimbleby & Shorland sold 600 of the Irish cattle in a single day and the firm began taking trainloads of Irish cattle throughout the country.

John Kirkwood so enjoyed the experience of these sales that in 1927 he joined the firm as an auctioneer and partner. At the same time as William Strang who had also worked for the Country Gentlemen's Association joined Thimbleby & Shorland along with a third colleague, Robert Habbitts, who would remain with the firm until the 1970s.

During this period most cattle were transported by rail and all the market drovers were on hand to take the cattle down the roads to Reading Station; as many readers will know the road between the railway bridge on Caversham Road and the Fire Station is still called Cattle Pens Road.

The expansion of the business continued with new partner John Kirkwood looking ever further afield; he realised that the best quality dairy cow was the Ayrshire from his native Scotland. Using the expertise gained from the Irish Store Cattle sales he arranged for a trainload of Ayrshires to come

Above: *The catalogue for the sale of equipment belonging to Billy Smart's Circus in 1986.*
Left: *A prize Jersey bull belonging to HM Queen Elizabeth fetched a UK record auction price of 3,200 guineas in October 1979.*

In 1934 however the partners in the firm were Lumley Thimbleby, son of the founder, John Kirkwood and William Strang. Their annual report for the previous year noted that business had begun badly in 1933 due to restrictions imposed as a response of a foot and mouth outbreak; but despite the trade in fat cattle being poor nevertheless fat pigs and fat sheep sold so well that by the end of the year the volume of stock handled by Thimbleby & Shorland was double what it had been in 1927.

The annual report made great emphasis on the store cattle sales indicating that since the sales of Irish cattle had begun in 1924 the firm had sold over a one and a half million pounds worth. In 1934 alone 26,466 Irish cattle would be sold at Reading. In addition Irish Cattle sales were held at St Ives, Ashford, Nottingham, Warminster, Dorchester, Leicester, Loughborough, Kettering, Worcester and Chelmsford - quite a feat for a small Reading firm to organise.

down from Glasgow. The first such sale was held in the Autumn of 1929. Most Englishmen had never seen cattle like them. By 1932 John Kirkwood was taking trainloads of Ayrshire cattle to all the main dairying areas of the country for sale. In December 1931 65 Ayrshire cattle were sold in Ashford Kent with a top price of 70 guineas for a three-year old heifer; in May of the following year 52 head were sold at York.

By 1935 prices had risen dramatically and the sale of the Studley certified herd of tuberculin tested milk recorded pedigree Ayrshire cattle at Ripon made the splendid average price of £30 4s 1d. And even bull calves made four guineas - a better price than at the end of the century!

During the 1930s sales continued in Reading Cattle Market with three firms now competing for the livestock business: WE Ross & Co., Simmons & Sons and Thimbleby & Shorland with FW Albright selling poultry. By the 1940s WE Scotchbrook had secured rights to sell the poultry in the market; Bill Scotchbrook, an ex-employee of Thimbleby & Shorland, would continue to sell poultry there until the late 1960s.

Richard Long came to the firm in 1947 after leaving the Royal Artillery where he had been a lance bombardier. Kerr Kirkwood joined the firm in 1949 and became a partner in 1957. John Holland and Michael Kimber both joined in the 1960s, becoming partners in 1975.

The famous Thimbleby & Shorland Reading Carriage Sales began in the 1960s under the guiding hand of John Mauger. John had joined the firm in 1957 and became a partner in the early 1960s. He realised that the growing sport of horse drawn carriage driving would create the need for specialist sales. Prior to then however the firm had of course frequently sold carriages. Back in 1912 a sale catalogue listed two brakes, two landaus, a brougham, a Victoria, a wagonette, three socia-bles, a dog cart, three station cabs, two hansoms and a strong spring trap - replacement by motor cars being the explanation for the sale.

Top: *A Heavy Horse Sale in 1979 where the top priced mare fetched 1,825 guineas.* ***Above:*** *Just one of the many carriages sold by the firm at their popular carriage sales.*

continues with the monthly Reading sales becoming more popular than ever under the guidance of partner, Richard Dance.

The other major change that Thimbleby & Shorland undertook was the introduction of Contractors Plant sales by John Holland, who with Richard Dance organises the five sales each year in Reading with entries of JCB diggers, excavators, dumpers, rollers, compressors, breakers and all the other items used in the construction business. The firm also conducts sales for major plant hire companies in the UK.

All through these periods of change the livestock market has continued even though numbers are lower than in the 1950s and 60s. Thimbleby & Shorland have maintained their commitment to serve the farming community by providing the right facilities for the farmer to trade his livestock. In the spring of 2001, foot and mouth again struck the countryside and all the livestock markets were closed and at the time of publication Thimbleby & Shorland were hoping that they would be reopen by the end of the summer.

Back in 1901 when the firm was founded, Mr Bailey held sales of furniture in Reading. Today, over one hundred years later, Thimbleby & Shorland are still holding monthly sales of furniture and fine art with many excellent pieces coming onto the market. These very large sales also have sections for computers, office furniture, small hand tools and DIY equipment, machine tools, motor vehicles and even growing plants! The local community flocks to these Saturday morning events.

Fancy a bid!

Top, both pictures: *Contractors Plant auction at Reading Market.* ***Below:*** *Farm dispersal sale held at Marlow.*

And some 30 years later Thimbleby & Shorland ran the sale of the Holywell Hackney Stud in Kent including many carriages not least the 'Tally Ho' road coach which sold for £150.

The real birth of the Thimbleby & Shorland carriage sales however came in the late 1950s when the firm sold the carriages of British Lion Films.

The first sale open to all vendors however came in 1965 and auctions have continued ever since with the first sale of the new millennium including more than 150 vehicles. In all some 20,000 carriages have passed through the firm's hands, selling to everyone from gypsies to the aristocracy.

By the millennium the Reading Carriage Sales, conducted by Thimbleby & Shorland partner Sarah Needham, had become an institution. Four times a year driving devotees would make their way to Reading to buy and sell carriages and equipment.

In 1969 Dick Long and Michael Kimber held the first Reading Shetland Pony sale with over 250 ponies from all over the country being entered. These sales have now by the millennium become the largest and most successful auction sales of Shetland ponies in the world, with buyers travelling from all over Europe and even North America to purchase the best bloodlines from the 450 ponies entered each time. During the 1970s many sales were held of pedigree horses and ponies including Welsh, hackney, spotted, palominos, Dartmoor and others. The tradition of Reading Market being a major centre for the horse trade

One of the world's great enterprises

For more than a quarter of a century the name of Foster Wheeler has been noted as one of the most prominent businesses based in Reading.

The UK arm of what is a huge international organisation was incorporated in 1920 when it employed just ten people and was known as the Power Specialty Company. Since its formation turnover has increased remarkably - from just £250,000 in 1930 until by the start of the

Millennium in the UK staff numbers had risen to 2,500 and annual turnover reached £600 million - and world-wide the company's turnover was being measured in billions of dollars.

It was in the USA that the Power Specialty Company had its roots. The Power Specialty Company of New York had been founded in 1900 by a group of young engineers previously connected with the Waterworks Supply Company which had been founded by the Foster family in 1884. The aim of the Power Specialty Company was to manufacture and sell hydraulic rams, fans for cooling towers, pump valves and steam heaters. By 1906 they had opened their first manufacturing plant in New York State and had offices in three American cities. By 1918 the company was applying its knowledge to oil refining and a new range of products was being developed .

Above: The Great Western Hotel, Reading, pictured towards the end of the 19th century. Below: The Power Specialty Company's first annual dinner in early 1923.

One of the firm's earliest orders for a compete distillation unit came from Shell, for its Vienna refinery. Within a year a similar order was placed for its Budapest refinery.

In a new move the company entered the vacuum refrigeration market with equipment for producing chilled water. The first order, in 1934, was for the air conditioning facilities for an oil company's hospital in Abadan, Iran. The same year equipment was supplied for air conditioning on the liners Queen Mary and the Empress of Britain. In 1935 Foster Wheeler supplied the largest vacuum refrigeration plant in the world to ICI for process work at Billingham.

The company received its first order to build a complete oil refinery in 1935 - to be built in Montevideo, Uruguay.

A British branch office was opened in 1919 at 315 Oxford Street, London, opposite the John Lewis store with a works in an ex-army hut in St Albans. The St Albans works however soon proved inadequate and a new works site was acquired at Egham, Surrey which would remain in use until the 1960s. In 1924 new offices were acquired, Aldwych House in the Strand, London, which would remain the company's headquarters for the following 25 years.

The war years took their toll on the company's headquarters at Aldwych House in London, which experienced serious bomb damage but they also saw the company involved in secret projects to help the war effort. The company assisted in the development and manufacture of 'hedgehogs' a multi-barrel mortar mounted on war ships for use against submarines, and FIDO (Fog Investigation Dispersal Operation) a unique fog dispersal system installed at RAF airfields which used petrol fired flame burners to heat air over the runways.

In 1927 a merger with the Wheeler Condenser Company, a firm founded in 1891 and which already shared at least two of its directors with Power Specialty, gave birth to Foster Wheeler Ltd; Foster being the surname of two of the group of young men who had founded the Power Specialty Company, Ernest and Pell Foster, and who were amongst its largest shareholders. Environmentally aware even in 1927 the original Power Specialty brass plate was put to maximum use: rather than buy a fresh plate for the new company name it was simply reversed and the new name engraved on the other side.

Nor were these the only contribution Foster Wheeler made to the war effort. From the early days of the war Foster Wheeler boilers were used in great numbers by the Royal Navy for sloops, steam gunboats, tank landing craft and destroyers. Later some of the firm's 'economisers' were fitted to larger ships including some aircraft carriers and Britain's last battleship HMS Vanguard.

Top left: The devastation outside Aldwych House following the rocket explosion in June 1944. Above: The company's name plaque with Foster Wheeler's name engraved onto the reverse of the Power Specialty Company's plaque. Right: Staff taking part in Foster Wheeler's Christmas party towards the end of the second world war.

In 1920 when the British company was formed its scale of activity was modest but by 1945, at the end of the second world war, the business began to expand rapidly becoming involved in contracts as diverse as refineries and steam generating plants. During that immediate post war period the company was responsible for building the largest oil refinery in Europe for Esso at Fawley on Southampton Water.

The Fawley project would take three years in the planning and the company would work there continuously for the next 25 years.

In those years there was also a massive ship building programme in Britain and no fewer than 17 ship yards were licensed to build Foster Wheeler D-type boilers. In fact two of these boilers

Top left: *The refinery at ICI Wilton.* ***Top right:*** *An early Foster Wheeler wagon.* ***Right:*** *The Jeremiah O'Brien powered by Foster Wheeler boilers.*

supplied by Foster Wheeler can still be seen today in the Boiler Room of the Royal Yacht Britannia which is moored at Leith, near Edinburgh.

With post-war expansion the Aldwych House offices became overcrowded. In 1950 it was decided to move to new headquarters at Ixworth Place, South Kensington where the firm would stay until 1960 when it would occupy Foster Wheeler House, a large tower block in Chapel Street, just off the Edgware Road, London before eventually moving, in October 1974, to Reading and a brand new Foster Wheeler House. This was a modern 10 storey office block on a site originally occupied by Vincents Garage opposite the railway station.

The 1950s saw much attention being paid to the generation of nuclear power. Foster Wheeler decided to concentrate on the use of nuclear power for submarines. Co-operation with Rolls Royce and Vickers eventually led to a joint company which carried out much of the work for the propulsion plant for the Royal Navy's first nuclear submarines.

Later, in the 1960s, the company built the largest coal-fired power station in Europe at Longannet for the South of Scotland Electricity Board. Five other major power stations were built for the Central Electricity Generating Board in England and Wales: at Tilbry, Aberthaw, Rugeley, Ironbridge and Eggborough.

The early 1970s would be dominated by the rapid build up of work related to North Sea oil. In 1973 the company was awarded its first major project in Norway for the Mongstad refinery. The following year the company began work on the largest oil and gas terminal

Additionally in the late 1990s, with leases for its central Reading offices expiring and ongoing growth in workload, Foster Wheeler took over the Berkshire County Council Headquarters at Shinfield Park. This has enabled the company to locate most of its Reading-based staff in one building and establish an effective centre for the 21st Century. The purchase was finalised in April 1998 and, following a major refurbishment programme, most staff have now relocated to Shinfield Park.

Today, from its small beginnings, Foster Wheeler, in the UK alone, has become a massive business in its own right and sponsors Foster Wheeler offices in

development in the world - the Sullom Voe terminal in the Shetlands where pipelines from the Brent and Ninian oil fields would terminate. That work would span ten years, and at its peak the workforce would number over 7,000.

Teesside, Glasgow, Johannesburg, Kuala Lumpur, Sriracha (Thailand) and Pudong (Shanghai) in China. It is part of one of the world's most prestigious engineering and construction groups with over a century of experience and dedicated, highly skilled personnel providing services in more than 35 countries on six continents. Those who work for the company in Reading can take pride in being part of a business which in more than a century has risen through the ranks to become one of the world's great enterprises.

Top left: Foster Wheeler at Shinfield Park. **Left:** *Foster Wheeler's former office in central Reading, Foster Wheeler House.* **Below:** *A liquefied natural gas facility in Oman.*

The largest load ever moved on Britain's public roads would be sent out from by Foster Wheeler in 1985. Eight abnormal loads were despatched to Shell's project at Stanlow; the largest load was 139 ft long, 52 ft in diameter and weighed over 600 tons; it was carried on a bogey with 26 axles each with 16 wheels.

During the 1970s and 1980s, the company won contracts in Canada, Kenya, Nigeria and Pakistan. In the UK, there were projects for ICI at Wilton, Shell at Stanlow and Roche Products and BP Chemicals in Scotland and BP at Wytch Farm, Dorset. A series of contracts for Glaxochem in Cumbria and Scotland were also won.

Since the 1990s, Foster Wheeler in the UK has worked on projects covering the various business sectors (oil and gas which include liquefied natural gas and gas-to-liquids; refining, chemicals, petrochemicals and polymers; pharmaceuticals; environmental and power) located in the UK, Europe, Africa, the Middle East, the Indian Subcontinent, South East Asia and China.

Shoppers' paradise

From sportswear and jewellery to musical instruments, mobile phones and computers fashions in shops, like fashions in clothes, change over the years. It does not seem too long ago that the vast majority of shops were owned by their management, individual owners ran single specialist shops - the butcher, the baker, and not forgetting the candlestick maker had their own names above the door with just a sprinkling of nationally known names punctuating the High Streets of Britain. Today the reverse is true and it sometimes seems that the national chains now predominate and the small family owned business is in the minority. And yet there remain some locations at least where 'owner occupiers' still predominate and where national chains still remain the icing rather than the cake.

Not that there is anything intrinsically wrong with nation-wide chain stores. At least the quality and standard of goods and service is the same wherever we go, though many mourn the passing of what, seen through rose tinted spectacles, still seems to have been a Golden Age.

But when did this change begin? Where can one start? Ask the question in a pub or café and the answers will vary from 'just after the war' to pointing the finger at the Victorians who not only seem to have invented the department store and the national chain but also gave us so many delightful market halls and shopping arcades.

Wherever one decides to draw the line however one will be wrong. Our townscapes are in a constant sate of flux. Sometimes that change is very gradual and sometimes much faster but, however slow or rapid, such evolution is unstoppable.

Above: *Broad Street in Victorian times.* ***Below:*** *Oxford Street, Reading in the 1930s.*

The Mall was created to fill the need for better shopping facilities in Reading town which had looked enviously at developments in other towns and been impressed by what was being done in the name of commercial progress.

The new building was constructed primarily in steel reinforced concrete on pillars, and in some areas with a moulded concrete platform. The whole structure was designed around a grid system which very often dictated the size of the shop units that would be used by the more than forty stores which would eventually come to occupy the building.

When first built the centre was known as 'The Butts Centre' a name associated with areas used in the Middle Ages for archery and other similar activities. Not surprisingly the name did not fail to raise a smile when Reading's ribald humorists also pointed out its other possible associations.

One of the periods of major change however for the whole country was the late 1960s and early 1970s. And Reading was no different to elsewhere in the UK. The winds of change were blowing round its shops too.

The Broad Street Mall was built around 1970. The building was designed by a company named Sidney Kaye, Eric Fermin & Partners on behalf of the Second Convent Garden Property Investment Company and Reading Borough Council.

After almost 20 years of use the name was changed when the building had a major internal refurbishment. That refurbishment included upgrading the mechanical services such as lifts and escalators in the building. The changes in what were described as the 'vertical transportation' in the

Top left: *Broad Street in the 1950s.* ***Above left:*** *The White Hart pub on Broad Street in 1966.*

building were also necessary to improve the public's access to the car park. The original design of the Mall's vertical transport made it difficult for the public to get to the second floor of the car park.

Over the years the Broad Street Mall has played host to such celebrities as Hunter from Gladiators, Fred Elliott and Sally Webster from Coronation Street and Cindy from Eastenders, each of whom has launched a Christmas season in the Mall. Choirs have performed, there have been

aerobics displays, Pepsi Challenges, art exhibitions, double glazing and conservatories erected and bathrooms and kitchens displayed. The management of the Mall likes to promote local charities such as the MS Therapy Centre, now based off the Oxford Road, and services like the National Blood Transfusion Service.

In recent times the Mall has hosted a knight in shining armour and his handmaiden presenting customers with roses throughout the day, whilst a Valentines Day featured romantic music played by pianist Tim Valentine. The Mall has also fielded a winning team in Reading's famous Charity Pancake Race and participated in the Reading half marathon, whilst St Patrick's Day has been celebrated with dancing fiddle players and blarney in the Circle Food Court combined with an opportunity to taste Guinness.

In fact anything that is happening in the community can and has been promoted within the Mall - and obviously these types of attractions help draw the public in.

The Circle Food Court which opened in 1992 proved to be very successful, with menus ranging from exotic Oriental meals to roasts, sausage and chips, ice-creams, baguettes and sandwiches. Naturally one of the aims of the Food Court was to encourage customers to spend longer in the Mall by enabling them to enjoy a relaxing meal during their 'shopping experience' and the six restaurants in one concept offering meals and snacks to suit all tastes from a deli and patisserie to Thai cuisine and traditional British fare would have something for everyone. At the time of writing the Circle Food Court was closed for extensive refurbishment and hopes to be reopened in time for Christmas 2001.

Naturally too the modern facilities at the Mall would include public toilets, a 'disabled toilet' (an expression which we all seem to have adopted despite the logical implication that it is the toilet itself which is disabled rather than the more accurate rendition 'a toilet for the disabled'), and a mother and baby changing room.

How things change. Another of the

Top left: *The modern exterior of the Broad Street Mall.* ***Left:*** *Inside the Broad Street Mall.*

hood of a fire; the Mall has a fully computerised fire alarm system which is entirely
automatic. And there are various devices
installed within the building to detect a fire
backed up by the team whose members are
constantly on patrol.

Times have indeed changed. Long gone is the
need to get wet whilst shopping dragging
small children by the hand listening to them
plaintively asking 'is it time to go home yet?'.
To our oldest residents who feel pangs of
nostalgia for the very old days however the
passing of such scenes may be mourned and
yet to many of those reading this book the
'new' shopping mall is now part of the old
days too. Many readers will not recall the
Mall having not been there; their memories
already include the Broad Street Mall as part
of their own childhoods and are now taking
their own children shopping to accumulate
their own memories of Reading.

What will today's youngsters recall, we
wonder, of their childhood shopping experiences with mum and dad? How will they
describe the Broad Street Mall and its
wonderful shops in decades to come when
their children and grandchildren in turn ask
them to talk about the good old days?

things which has changed over the years has been our
increasing interest in safety. A Security Department plays
a very important role in the running of the Mall. Security
Officers on patrol during the day and night are backed up
by closed circuit television cameras with a recording
facility allowing the Mall's staff to refer back to any
incident at a later time. The Mall's Security Officers are
trained in the aspects of law and order although
they have no more powers than that of citizen's
arrest. Staff have the right to refuse entry into the
building just as each of us has the power to refuse
admission into our homes. Security staff do
sometimes have a difficult job to do, but with
careful training and guidance the team can cope
with anything.

And should a tenant be involved with a shoplifter a
Security Officer will assist the tenant in dealing with
the situation. Ultimately however when an offence is
committed the police will be involved.

Allied to security in the building is safety. The
security team is trained in what to do in the event of
fire or other incident. Not that there is much likeli-

The Broad Street Mall has succeeded in combining the best
aspects of traditional shopping with the finest modern
standards. Surely no mean feat?

Top left: *Christmas celebrations with guest Sally
Whittaker who plays Sally Webster in Coronation Street.*
Below: *The celebrated Circle Food Court.*

Moving times

The Robert Darvall Group, the Reading-based group of removal companies, traces its origins to the 1920s, and to local man Robert Darvall.

Robert Darvall was a coal and coke merchant running his business using a single horse and cart. The business started out based in Whitley Wood Lane, where the firm would continue to be located for more than 50 years.

Robert's wife, Edith, also took a very active role in the business. Not only did Edith run the office, but during peak periods was often seen filling coal sacks.

The 1920s were lean years for the whole country, and Reading was no exception. The 1930s would be even worse with a great world-wide economic recession following the Wall Street Crash, plunging the British economy into a downward spiral from which few would escape. Despite those hard times however, those who provided the necessities of life were able to survive a little better than most. No-one could do without food and so small shop keepers such as butchers and bakers could ride out the storm - and similarly those who sold coal and coke, the fuel which in the days before smokeless zones and central heating kept us all warm in our homes.

Not many of us, save the oldest, now recall the coal man's horse and cart piled high with sacks ready to be delivered down our streets. But those of us who are middle aged still recall with surprising happiness the sight of the coal delivery wagon, its flat bed laden with full sacks to be lifted on to the shoulders of a burly and black faced young, and sometimes not so young, man to be dropped into our coal cellars and bunkers. Do you remember how the sacks would be laid out on the pavement afterwards to be counted by the householder to check that just the right number had been delivered?

Above: The vehicle bought by Ken when he joined the firm in 1965. Below: The firm's premises in the mid 1970s.

the Company, Lisa, Simon and Gareth and more recently a fourth generation family member, Matthew, Simon's son, has joined the business.

The firm would move to the site of its present headquarters in Acre Road only in 1978.

Ken Darvall had spent nine years in the police before leaving the force and buying lorry RVE 532 to begin a general Haulage and Removal Service.

By the 1980s the firm had grown remarkably. In 1988 the company purchased two new vehicles: the first a £42,000 32 tonne Supercube Mercedes truck, the second a 1926 Morris Commercial!

The Mercedes would go to join the fleet of 20 vehicles and the innumerable trailers which Ken Darvall, now Managing Director, was running at full tilt to keep pace with the growing national and international business.

Meanwhile the Morris Commercial, believed to be the last in existence, would represent what Ken hoped would be the first in a collection of old time vehicles.

Pending the creation of such a collection the by-then-62 year old 12 seater was pressed into service at charity

And unlike many other businesses the advent of the second world war would have little impact on the small firm - coal and coke deliveries being vital to the nation.

Robert and Edith's son Maurice joined the firm in 1946 as a general helper and arranged for the purchase of the firm's first lorry.

Moving timber and furniture were soon added to the firm's activities. The latter activity leading to one more step forward with the purchase of a canvas sheet to cover furniture in transit.

Like her mother-in-law before her Maurice's wife, Joyce Darvall, would help her husband by working in the firm's office. In 1965 Ken, Maurice's younger brother, joined the business and was assisted by his first wife Di, who helped run the office. Subsequently three of their children joined

Top: *Company vehicles in the 1960s.* **Above:** *Another view of the yard in the 1970s.*

team which would plan every last detail including the technical and legal implications of moving, the protection and preservation of IT investments, staff health and safety, a moving and re-installation strategy, equipment testing and aftercare - and even advice on how to ensure that productivity in the organisation could quickly return to pre-move levels.

And not only that. Almost every move brings with it a host of excess or unwanted items which need to be stored or disposed of. That is where the large warehouse storage facilities at Business Moves came into play - clients' documents and archives could be stored until needed and any old or unwanted equipment and files could be disposed of. Security shredding of sensitive documents was carried out and certified within 24 hours whilst cleaning services were organised, to prepare new offices or to restore vacated offices to meet any outstanding contractual arrangements.

events around Berkshire where Ken was a Rotary Club fund raising officer.

The Morris had been used on the service between Horndean in Sussex and Portsmouth, but because of Darvall's close association with Reading Transport the firm changed its livery from blue to red and white, the local bus company's original colours.

Moving into Europe was not without its difficulties, not least when on the firm's first trip to Spain the wrong paperwork resulted in one of the company's vans being stranded on the border with Spain for two weeks until the mess was sorted out by the Spanish Foreign Ministry. Such problems would not however occur again.

Office moving throughout Europe led not only to a major period of expansion but also to a recognition that the company's future lay not with its now traditional base of home removals but with the commercial sector. That realisation would lead in due course to a management buy-out of the domestic arm of the company which would subsequently be run as a separate business.

The key to the growth of the Darvall group's Business Moves company was an understanding of customers' needs. Just like any other business activity office relocation needs clearly defined objectives. Moving an office to another location, whether within the same building or to a distant location, demands a level of skill and management which can overburden even the most well prepared office managers, at a time when the demands on them are already very high indeed. Business Moves developed a Moving Plan for each client which would be well organised and cost effective; the company also provided a relocation

Another arm of the business would be records management. Information storage and management is a challenge to all businesses, large or small. Records are a valuable commodity and must be carefully maintained and

Top left: *Ken and Maurice studying a map of Spain.*
Below: *Ken, Simon and Gareth outside the premises circa 1990. The 1926 Morris Commercial is pictured behind them.*

Important customers include Compaq, Hewlett Packard, the Halifax Bank, Bradford and Bingley Building Society, Oracle, Yellow Pages and HSBC.

Now in the 21st century the firm aims to be recognised as the nation's number one 'turn key' service provider to the commercial relocation market, not only for the service it offers but also for its business morals and ethics. The intention is to build a nationwide and European network and, through efficient management and operating systems and technology, offer a total and cost effective service throughout the UK and Europe, working with clients to constantly seek new ways to meet their needs and improve its services.

Simon Darvall, current Managing Director, is keen to heap praise on the fantastic input past and present employees have had in the Company's growth. Aiming to set the standard to which all others aspire, this innovative, family-owned group of businesses demonstrates yet again that even the most modest of small businesses can, with time, dynamic leadership and ambitious plans eventually grow to become a major undertaking.

documented, sometimes for long periods and taking up valuable time, space and human resources. The need to track and code each individual item for quick retrieval however is paramount. This was why Business Records Management with its long history of records retrievals as part of the Robert Darvall Group was able to offer a unique service. Business Records Management could offer a network of secure storage centres around UK. The business would adhere to strict standards for the protection and safekeeping company data, employing sophisticated logging and tracking software to combine accurate cataloguing and monitoring facilities with a programmable retrieval and delivery service, to meet client's demands. Physical security would be provided at all storage centres with 24 hour surveillance systems and the bar-coding of all storage files and boxes removed the need for visible text labelling.

Today Business Moves Ltd's main markets remain office and commercial moving and IT installations. Depots are found not only at the group's head office in Reading but also in Bristol, Leeds, London, Manchester, Milton Keynes, Edinburgh and Glasgow.

*Top: The fleet in the 1990s. **Above left:** one of the Business Moves vehicles. **Below:** Robert Darvall Group Ltd's head office.*

Full steam ahead

For over half a century the GH Marshall Ltd company name has been synonymous with quality mechanical services; those services are provided to clients representing a wide spectrum of local industry and commerce.

The business, established in 1949, was originally based in London Street before eventually moving to its current premises at 10 Carey Street in 1952. The Carey Street site occupies around half an acre of land which was once Drakes' market garden and nursery.

George Henry Marshall founded the business with Henry Graham; they subsequently registered the firm as a limited company in 1951.

GH Marshall was a steam engineer and because of that the company had a strong steam bias in the early days. The trend however soon moved away from steam as a main source of energy, though the company still prides itself on its steam capabilities.

During the 1950s and 60s the company had a social club which arranged day trips for staff to the south coast; the practice has now disappeared as most staff now have personal transport for their leisure pursuits. Marshall's recruitment and training policy of taking three or four craft apprentices each year had meant that, especially in the 1970s when training still involved a five year course, up to 20 young people were being trained at anyone time. During the first 50 years of the firm's history it could boast of having trained over 130 apprentices. Taking school leavers in this way has meant that some employees have stayed with the company for 30 years or more.

During the 1960s and 70s Marshall's had a highly successful local football team originally made up of players from its staff, many of whom were apprentices. Today Marshall's is still sponsoring local youth teams.

During the 1950 and 60s the decline of steam coupled with an increase in available labour had meant that the company was able to diversify into other markets such as site maintenance and general heating and ventilation. Continued growth over the years meant that by the early 1970s Marshall's was employing a staff of over 70 and

*Above: Mr GH Marshall and Mrs Gladys Marshall at the Great Western Hotel, Reading, celebrate the firm's silver Anniversary in 1974. **Below:** Staff pose for the camera before one of the many trips organised by the company during the 1950s and 60s.*

passed away in 1981. Pamela Brownlow suceeded Gladys Marshall as Company Secretary in 1980 and continued in that position until 1997, whilst Joan Hall and Malcolm Marshall both joined the Board of Directors in 1988.

Changes to the management structure in the late 1980s saw the appointment of Geoff Brown as Managing Director who divided the company into three main sections: Contracts, Maintenance and Small Works.

The Contracts Division took on all major new build or refurbishment projects within the building services industry up to the value of a million pounds. This also gave clients the option of a maintenance contract with the Maintenance Division once any warranty period expired.

The Maintenance Division would come to hold many of the maintenance contracts for MoD sites in the locality.

The Small Works Division was set up to deal with smaller specialist projects and to give a rapid response to such things as boiler replacement and general repairs.

By the millennium annual turnover had reached seven million pounds. Clients would include not only many local schools but also such prestigious sites as the Royal Household, Thames Valley Police, the University of Reading, Oxford University, Reading Old Town Hall, the Royal Military Academy at Sandhurst, the Royal Berks Hospital, Reading Prison and St Mary's Butts church, the BBC and IBM.

achieving an annual turnover of half a million pounds. George Henry had nurtured the business from its humble beginnings into one of the most successful mechanical service providers in the area.

The company's 21st anniversary in 1970 and its 25th in 1974 were both marked by celebrations at the Great Western Hotel in Reading. All employees and many of the company's clients attended.

George Henry Marshall had four children all of whom at some stage worked for the company; two of whom, Malcolm Marshall and Mrs Joan Hall, would still be directors more than 50 years after the firm's founding. George Henry had eventually taken a back seat in the company and handed over the reins to his eldest son George David, who continued until 1988. Sadly George Henry Marshall

Top left: Staff on a trip during the 1950s.
Above left: Pausing for a picnic on route to the south coast in the 1950s. Below: Company vehicles, 2001.

Keeping the books

Accountancy has been with us for a long time. No-one can pinpoint its precise origins; but no doubt the Ancient Egyptians needed to keep a tally of work on their pyramids and the Romans to keep accurate records of tax gathering. Double entry bookkeeping had its beginnings in the counting houses of renaissance Venice . The earliest text on accountancy in English was written by Hugh Oldcastle, a London schoolmaster who taught arithmetic and bookkeeping, and published in 1543.

Not quite as old as the 16th century, but still long established, the Ernest Francis accountancy firm has built an enviable reputation for helping a wide range of private, commercial, professional and non-commercial clients. Those clients range from individuals to multi-million pound organisations in the Thames Valley and North Hampshire areas. Whatever their size all clients are assured of the personal attention of a partner and senior staff who know and understand their circumstances. But when did this prestigious local firm first appear in Reading?

The story begins in 1888 with Ernest Francis working in partnership with one Samuel Preston. Preston had been Clerk to the Reading, Earley and Tilehurst School Boards and had himself earlier been in partnership with a Mr J Egginton practising as auctioneers, accountants and estate agents. Egginton had opened his first office as an accountant in 1864 and become the Government Auditor for Berkshire and Oxfordshire, enabling today's firm by that count to trace its furthest origins to 1864.

From 1888 however Samuel Preston went his own way whilst Ernest Francis carried on the former practice in his own name from 150, Friar Street.

Around 1890 the one-man firm moved again this time to 38, Friar Street, the auctioneering side of the practice ceased and eventually any association with estate agency also fell by the wayside.

In 1880 the Institute of Chartered Accountants had been incorporated by Royal Charter and it was possible for practising accountants to be become members by application only. Ernest Francis was admitted a member on 5th February 1896 and his certificate of membership, No 2297, is still held in the present firm's office. By 1899 the practice had moved to 172, Friar Street.

Top left: The firm's founder, Ernest Francis. **Below:** *Friar Street in the 1880s where Ernest started his business.*

Today, run from Oswald House in Queens Road, the firm of Ernest Francis - having now lost the '& Son' - is large enough to cope with the most complex issues, yet still small enough to care about each individual client. The staff of 40, many of whom have a long connection with the firm, offer a range of expertise and services more often associated with far larger firms. Their commitment to providing every client with a high quality service is evidenced by the firm's membership of the CharterGroup partnership, a national network of independent accountancy firms, membership of which is conditional upon meeting stringent quality requirements.

In 1921, Oswald Francis, after a distinguished career in the Royal Berkshire regiment during the first world war, joined his father in the practice and remained a partner until his retirement in 1961; he had served the community in many ways and had been appointed Chairman of the Reading Bench. From 1921, when Oswald joined his father, the firm would become known as Ernest Francis & Son.

The firm would move to 8, The Forbury in 1934 and remain there until 1972 when a move was made to Somerset House in Blagrave Street.

Throughout the years the firm of Ernest Francis & Son maintained close ties with the Francis family; even a whole century after its founding, in 1988, the then senior partner John Tovey was related to the Francis family by marriage.

For many local businesses and professions of all kinds Ernest Francis & Son through the firm's great experience, local knowledge and comprehensive range of professional services has looked after the books for generations. The firm has had a long association with Reading and the surrounding district through the extensive involvement of its partners, past and present, in local sporting and community affairs. It remains one of the oldest established accountancy practices in Reading and also has a long-standing association with Basingstoke and North Hampshire through its busy and successful office in that town which opened in 1956.

Top left: *The partners of the firm with the Mayor of Reading and the Deputy Mayor of Basingstoke on the occasion of the firm's 110th Anniversary, at the Old Town Hall, Reading.* ***Above right:*** *Two of the firm's staff on duty on the occasion of the firm's 110th Anniversary. They are giving away bottles of Ernest Francis "own label" claret to all their guests.* ***Above left:*** *Partners Richard Rand, and Graham Carter, with members of staff in the firm's Reading Office Conference Room.* ***Below:*** *Blagrave Street, where the firm moved to in 1972 and then left for their present Queen's Road premises in 1995.*

Metals - but not as we know them

In 1817 Percival Norton Johnson set up as an assayer and gold refiner and in 1822 moved to premises in Hatton Garden, London. He quickly gained a reputation for accuracy and backed this by offering to purchase the gold bars he assayed. Soon a small gold refinery was established, which later was extended to handle platinum and palladium. In 1838, at the age of 13, George Matthey joined Johnson as an apprentice. In 1845, George Matthey took charge of the platinum laboratory and in 1851 the partnership of Johnson & Matthey was formed. As a result of their skill and integrity, in 1852 they were appointed official Assayer to the Bank of England.

From an early stage in the company's history it developed a special interest and expertise in platinum. The company developed methods for platinum fabrication and a practical method for the melting of platinum which operated well into the 20th century was established. George Matthey also developed the fusion welding of platinum to produce reliable joints. As a result Johnson Matthey became specialists in the manufacture of the platinum boilers used in the manufacture and concentration of sulphuric acid. These early developments formed the basis for the industrial applications of platinum which are the primary interest of the company to this day. During the second world war Johnson Matthey

products played a very significant part in the allied war effort and after the war the Company enjoyed a great period of growth.

In the late 1960s in the UK scientists and engineers at Johnson Matthey developed catalyst technology based on platinum group metals to control gaseous pollutants from industrial plants. In the 1970s, clean air legislation forced vehicle manufacturers to investigate ways of reducing emissions from cars. Johnson Matthey successfully demonstrated the benefits of their platinum-based catalyst in reducing car exhaust pollution, and the day of the catalytic converter had come. This resulted in the opening at Royston in 1974 of the world's

Top right: *Transporting materials at Hatton Garden in the 1920s.* ***Left:*** *The Wembley premises, home of the Research Laboratories until 1975.*

The Centre was pivotal in the research and development of new platinum-based anti-cancer drugs which are now widely used in cancer chemotherapy. Johnson Matthey received its second Queen's Award for Technological Research for its research in this area, jointly with the Institute of Cancer Research and the Royal Marsden Hospital. In 2001 the Royal Society of Chemistry awarded its first National Historic Chemical Landmark to the Johnson Matthey Technology Centre to recognise its chemical research into the platinum group metals, and the life enhancing applications of that research.

Johnson Matthey is continuing its tradition of research and innovation. A key area of research today is fuel cell technology, which is aimed at the development of a clean source of power for the new millennium.

Top left: *The laboratories at Blount's Court in the 1970s.*
Top right: *The laboratories after the completion of a major extension in 1990.*
Above left: *The house at Blount's Court.*
Below: *Fuel test facility.*

first production plant for the manufacture of catalytic converters and the Company received the first of two Queen's Awards for Technological Achievement.

The increasing importance of research and development in the 1970s led to the establishment of the Johnson Matthey Technology Centre at Blount's Court, Sonning Common, Berkshire. The company's research laboratories had previously been based at Wembley in North London. The history of Blount's Court dates back to 1287 when a certain Ralph Pippard granted land to John Kent. In 1465, the house became the residence of Thomas Stonor and it remained in the Stonor family until the early 18th century. Subsequent owners were Charles Price, Thomas Ovey, Colonel T Knollys and the Peel family. In 1960 the building was sold to the American Machine Foundry Ltd for conversion into laboratories. In 1964 Brook Bond Tea Ltd purchased the property. Finally in 1975, Johnson Matthey acquired Blount's Court. Since that time, the company has extended the laboratories and today nearly 200 people are employed at the site.

From kitchen range to complete building supply range

D rew's The Ironmongers is one of Reading's best known family businesses. In living memory the town hosted more than 40 ironmongery stores as well as numerous tool and hardware shops. Many of those firms have closed and since the arrival of the DIY superstores Drews isalmost unique in the town as an independent hardware store.

Trained as a plumber, Percy John Drew was a manager for Callas Son & May, general ironmongers in Oxford Road, Reading. He did not see eye to eye with Mr Tommy May who 'sacked' Percy on numerous occasions. Having been told to collect his cards just once too often, he left in 1920. He called on Perris Brothers (Estate Agents) who had a kitchen range that needed repairing. He borrowed a hand truck and took it to a yard in Minster Street belonging to Fullers paint merchants, repaired it and took it back. Percy was in business!

Unfortunately little else is known of the following years of trading but something that is certain from this time is that

Above: Percy Drew (the Founder) top right, Archie Drew, top left and David Drew on his Great-grandfather's knee.
Below: Staff behind the counter in the 1970s.
Right: Reg Ayres behind the trade counter.

in 1929 whilst trading from Queens Road, P J Drew became a limited company. It is thought that at one time the company employed 50 plumbers, 2 bricklayers, a blacksmith, 2 tinsmiths and a locksmith.

In 1931 'Drews' acquired premises on the corner of Friar Street and Greyfriars Road. Soon after this the workshop in Queens Road was relocated to Caversham Road and the 'yard' opened in Vachel Road to store some of the heavy or bulky products.

Percy Drew was something of a remote individual and ran the business single-handed. When he died in 1956, his son, Archie Drew, took over knowing nothing of the financial side of the business. This was a very difficult time for him, to his credit business flourished.

Archie soon realised that the workshop side of the business was not very profitable and closed the Caversham Road location to concentrate on retail, selling to both tradesmen and the DIY customer the

In recent years the fourth generation of the Drew family, Chris, Nic and Lisa Drew have joined the company.

In the face of increased competition in both the trade and DIY markets, the business has continued to grow such that Drews now boasts an annual turnover in excess of £2 million. There is still room in the marketplace for the specialist supplier that stocks products in depth, offers expert and personal service and is prepared to source products not kept on the shelf - qualities on which Drews' excellent reputation is founded.

Indeed Drews' reputation stretches far and wide with regular customers in the Hebrides, Jersey, France, the Seychelles and even Australia turning to Drews for items they require. Most of Drews' customers, however, are local with many of Reading's major building contractors, schools, the Council, hospitals and university among their account holders - though Drews pride themselves on giving the same high level of attention to each customer and each order regardless of size.

products that remain the core of the business to this day: ironmongery, locks, tools, fixings and plumbing supplies.

In 1963 Archie's son, David Drew (the present Managing Director) joined the company. David and Archie realised that larger premises with easier access were needed and so began a fifteen year search that ended when, in 1979, Drew's moved to their present premises on Caversham Road.

The old Friar Street shop may have had a certain charm and appeal to the public but it posed numerous difficulties for the staff. Most of the stock was in the cellars and to serve one customer often involved several trips up and down the stairs - the only blessing of this arrangement was that when there was a particularly difficult customer staff could vent their feelings out of earshot!

The new premises offered self-selection facilities and customer parking, both essential for Drews to compete with 'out of town superstores'.

Whilst apart from a few technical innovations the products sold have not changed too much over time, but the way they are sold certainly has. There is now a computerised point of sale system and the company has two internet sites, www.pjdrew.co.uk and www.bootsforwork.com which have helped gain national exposure for the company and securing them orders from places far distant from their Reading base.

Top left: The firm's premises in the 1970s.
Above left: Max Mawer in the stockroom.
Below: The firm's premises in 2001.

Acknowledgments

The publishers would like to thank
Reading Central Library and
Matthew Williams, Reading Museum

Thanks are also due to
Andrew Mitchell who penned the editorial text
and Steve Ainsworth and Judith Dennis for their copywriting skills